This book was made possible through
the generous assistance of:

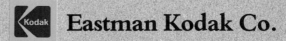 Eastman Kodak Co.

SONY.

Intourist

Yuri Abramochkin

David C. Turnley

First published 1987 by Collins Publishers, Inc. New York.

Copyright © 1987 by Collins Publishers, Inc.

ISBN 0-00-217972-5

Library of Congress Cataloging-in-Publication Data.
Main entry under title: A Day in the life of the Soviet Union.

1. Soviet Union—Description and travel—1970—Views.
2. Soviet Union—Social life and customs—1970—
Pictorial works.
I. Smolan, Rick.
II. Cohen, David, 1955–

DK18.5.D39 1987
947.085′4′0222   87-1838-1

Project Directors: Rick Smolan and David Cohen

Art Director: Thomas K. Walker

Cover photograph shot on Kodachrome film by Larry C. Price

Printed in Japan   First printing August 1987

10   9   8   7   6   5   4   3   2   1

A Day in the Life of the Soviet Union

**Photographed by 100 of the
world's leading photojournalists
on one day, May 15, 1987**

Collins Publishers
in association with Ira Shapiro

Alma Ata, 6:30 a.m.: A woman sweeps the podium stairs at
Brezhnev Square.

Leningrad, 7:15 a.m.: Cadets at the Nakhimov Navel Academy jog
along the banks of the Neva River.

Vladivostok, 7:30 a.m.: Sunrise over Golden Horn Bay.

Fog shrouds the icy waters of the Bering Sea on May 15, 1987, and youngsters collect on the shore to wait for their fishermen fathers to bring
in the catch. Beyond the mist, 70 miles away, lies America—the Aleutian
Islands. Far, far to the west, nearly 7,000 miles distant in Soviet Kaliningrad
(the Königsberg of pre-war East Prussia), families are now sitting down to dinner.
There, it is the night before, May 14th. They are closer to the USA than to the
Bering shores.

The sheer distances are breathtaking. On that same day in May, women are setting out tomatoes in the Qara Qum Desert, perspiring in temperatures that hover
around 100°F. A half-continent to the north in Dickson, high above the Arctic
circle, the temperature has risen from a winter low of − 70°F to 32°F. Summer is
at hand.

The Soviet Union is a land of extremes. In the Czar's day, the monarch was
proclaimed sovereign of "all the Russias." Anyone turning the pages of *A Day
in the Life of the Soviet Union* can see why. Was there ever a realm so diverse,
so enriched by differing peoples, cultures and geography? Even the Roman
Empire pales by comparison.

In 40 years of travel across these endless steppes, tundras, forests and mountains, I thought I had seen it all. But in 40 minutes with this book, I discovered
more than I have in thousands upon thousands of miles of reporting on Russia.

Here I found places and people no Americans (and few Russians) have ever
seen—the inside of Vladimir Prison, the dread "Isolator" of Aleksandr
Solzhenitsyn's *The Gulag Archipelago,* a dungeon where men and women in
the not distant past suffered in cold and dark and damp for years until death came
as a blessing. The photographs, taken by Pulitzer Prize-winning American photographer, Eddie Adams, look more like army fatigue shots than scenes from
Solzhenitsyn's *One Day in the Life of Ivan Denisovich.* Never mind, they are a
remarkable first.

A Day in the Life of the Soviet Union gives us Russia without tears, Russia
without the cloak of censorship—well, almost without that cloak. There are
many spots it does not penetrate. But it is only thanks to Mikhail Gorbachev's
glasnost policy that the book can scan the life of Soviet citizens in this uninhibited
fashion. Almost all of Russia is here, the bad along with the good.

The rich texture of this work astonishes someone like myself who has experienced Russia in so many modes—the desperate savagery of the Nazi invasion
of World War II, the last days of Stalin's terror, the turbulent Khrushchev reforms
and the galvanic era of Gorbachev. Here are the eternal countrymen out of

Millet and Breughel. Here, too, are leather-jacketed dudes straight from *A Clockwork Orange*—only these toughs inhabit Arctic Yakutsk rather than swinging London. And here are weightless cosmonauts girding for life in space at Star City outside Moscow—another first, this photograph. And a shot of the control panel of one of Chernobyl's nuclear twins, its cutoff switches guarded by wax seals and cords reminiscent of the time of Catherine the Great.

We glimpse Russia past, Russia present, Russia future. We gaze at a young woman who could be Anna Karenina. Two of Chekov's *Three Sisters* talk quietly on a park bench; candle-lit worshippers pray in an Orthodox church. An old general who might have fought Napoleon in 1812 dozes behind his bemedaled chest. A shy lad wanders in from the Christmas party in *The Nutcracker*. Young ballet pupils dream of becoming the Anna Pavlova of the year 2001.

General Secretary Mikhail Gorbachev, with Foreign Minister Schevardnadze, is captured in a fleeting moment in his Kremlin office. Vignettes of the by-products of *glasnost* appear on almost every page: there are private market traders and a very Russian spinoff, muscle freaks who call themselves Lyubers, after Lyubertsy, their hard-hat suburban Moscow stronghold. (Lyubertsy grew up around the pre-Revolutionary factory of Chicago's International Harvester Company.) These bodybuilders are bodybusters—they beat up hippies, punks and heavy-metal types, coming on like Hell's Angels.

Russia is people. The people on these pages may aspire to America's consumer society, but they want their own version: no carbon copies, please.

One hundred and fifty years ago Gogol asked in *Dead Souls:*

Russia, are you not speeding along like a fiery and matchless troika? Beneath you the road is smoke, the bridges thunder and everything is left far behind. . . . Russia, where are you flying? . . . The air is torn and thundering as it turns to wind; everything on earth comes flying past and, looking askance at her, other peoples and states move aside and make way.

The *troikas* are gone but the world is still wondering where Russia is speeding to. Gogol's words are those of a poet. Perhaps through the remarkable *A Day in the Life of the Soviet Union* we can find new and better clues to where Russia has arrived and gain some notion of where she is headed.

A Day in the Life of the
SOVIET UNION

March 1, 1987

Dear Photographer,

I'm an American freelance photographer, and for the past ten years I've been working on assignments around the world for magazines including *Newsweek*, *Time*, *Fortune*, The London *Sunday Times*, *Stern* and *National Geographic*. I'm writing to invite you to work on a project that David Cohen and I are organizing here in Moscow.

This is what we have in mind: We want to position 100 of the world's best photographers (50 Western and 50 Soviet-bloc) throughout the Soviet Union and give each photographer the same 24-hour period to capture a typical Soviet day on film. The result of this shoot will be a hardcover book called, "A Day in the Life of the Soviet Union."

During the past three years we have had many meetings and much correspondence with Soviet officials in Moscow and Washington seeking permission to bring the world's leading photographers to the Soviet Union. Each time, we were politely rebuffed. The concept of letting 100 photojournalists loose in the USSR seemed to be an idea which the Soviets could never accept. Last fall, however, after "A Day in the Life of America" hit the number 1 position on the New York Times best-seller list, we received a call from the Soviet Embassy saying they were ready to discuss the possibility of "A Day in the Life of the Soviet Union" more seriously.

The U.S.S.R has undergone an extraordinary transformation in the past year in response to General-Secretary Gorbachev's glasnost (openness) policy. The Western photographers who work on "A Day in the Life of the Soviet Union" will be given unprecedented access to previously taboo subjects and closed areas. Still, we will be walking a tightrope while making this book. People will expect "A Day in the Life of the Soviet Union" to be either a whitewash showing only good aspects of the country or a diatribe against the Soviets. If we are successful, our book won't fall into either category. Like previous "Day in the Life" books, the Soviet effort should present nothing more or less than the daily life of the people. If any conclusions are to be drawn, they should be drawn by our readers who will be free to decide for themselves what these pictures say about the Soviet people.

"A Day in the Life of the Soviet Union" must first and foremost be a superior photographic document that answers a few questions about the Soviet Union and perhaps asks a few more. The project is also designed, however, to provide a group of talented individuals with the opportunity to work together on a collaborative project and to allow you and the other photojournalists to share the camaraderie which has characterized previous "Day in the Life" projects.

Unlike our previous books, "A Day in the Life of the Soviet Union" must somehow capture an area 5 times the size of the United States, an area which encompasses 15 republics, each with its own culture, language and customs. To create, in only one day, a cohesive book that accurately represents the lives of these heterogeneous people is going to be a nearly impossible task.

On Sunday, May 10, 1987, you and colleagues from 20 countries will arrive in Moscow. On Friday, May 15, 1987, each of you will photograph a specific aspect of Soviet life. All over the country, 100 photographers will race against the clock to freeze this previously unphotographable country on film during the course of a single day. We will give each of you a specific assignment, but you will also be allowed to shoot whatever you discover by accident on the day. The assignment is just a starting point.

Remember, though, we are not setting out to make the definitive statement about the Soviet Union or to cover the entire country in a single day. Instead, we will ask you to apply your skills to one of the toughest jobs in photojournalism: to make extraordinary photographs of ordinary, everyday events.

Although this project is made possible by Eastman Kodak, Pan American Airlines, Nikon Cameras, Sony and Intourist, all the supporters of this project understand that you are a journalist and that they will have no editorial control over what you shoot or what is selected for the book. Each of you will have a guide, but they have been instructed to let you shoot freely. We want "A Day in the Life of the Soviet Union" to be an honest look at the Soviet Union in the 1980s, not just another book of model farms, factories and families. By the same token, there is no guarantee that every photographer will get a picture in the book. That depends on whether or not you have a good day on May 15th.

At the moment, we have staffs in Moscow, Madrid and New York all frantically putting the last pieces in place to make sure everything goes smoothly when you and the other photographers arrive here. If working with us on this crazy idea appeals to you, here are a few things you will need to know and a few things we need from you very quickly:

1) **Biography:** Don t be modest. We need as much information as possible about your photography career -- awards, exhibits, books published, etc.

2) **Film:** Kodak will supply you with 50 rolls of film (Kodachrome 64 or 200 or T-MAX-400). It would help us to know your film requirements in advance.

3) **International Transportation:** You will receive a round-trip Pan Am ticket from your home city to Moscow.

4) **Domestic Transportation:** You will be provided with Aeroflot flights, a Novosti assistant and translator and a car and driver.

5) **Roommates:** If you take advantage of the hotel rooms provided to you at the Intourist Hotel, you will share a twin room with a famous photographer at absolutely no extra charge.

6) **Payment:** All expenses including air and ground travel will be covered by us. In return for the one day of shooting, you have the choice of receiving either a cash honorarium of $500 or a Sony 8mm Handycam video camera. You will also receive a Nikon auto-focus 20/20 camera with a 35-70mm zoom lens.

There is no question that this project will be the most challenging one we've attempted to date. The logistics are daunting, to say the least, and we are more than aware how fragile this project is. An international incident could easily jeopardize everything. We are being allowed unprecedented access, and there will be a tremendous amount of world attention focused on this project. We are not certain that the success we have enjoyed with our first five books can be repeated in a country that has never been known for its openness to photographers. This is why we need people of your caliber and experience.

We hope you will be able to lend your skills, and believe you will be as fascinated with the Soviet Union as we are.

Best regards,

Rick Smolan

Jay Dickman

● *Previous page*

Mariya Gerasimenko herds her geese at Poltava's Druzhba (Friendship) Horse Farm in Ukraine. Having reached pension age, Gerasimenko has retired from her work in the collective farm's fields, and she can sell the eggs and meat from her fowl for a small profit. In Ukrainian, chickens and ducks are called by saying "*tsyp, tsyp, tsyp,*" while geese answer to "*tega, tega.*"
Photographer:
Jay Dickman, USA

● *Above*

An old woman waters plants in the entrance hall of the Nakhimov Naval Academy in Leningrad.
Photographer:
David Hume Kennerly, USA

● *Right*

A caretaker keeps Lenin's final resting place spotless, while a KGB honor guard stands watch. Lenin's symbolic importance is signified by the mystery and authority accorded his remains.

Lenin receives millions of visitors each year. They line up two abreast and solemnly circle the Soviet founding father's glass sarcophagus before exiting to pay their respects to the pantheon of Soviet leaders buried along the back wall of the Kremlin.
Photographer:
Larry C. Price, USA

● *Left*

A Soviet border guard checks the identification papers of an Eskimo hunter. Times have changed for the indigenous peoples of the Far East. Their traditional hunting grounds in the Bering Sea have become a highly sensitive, heavily patrolled border area between the United States and the Soviet Union. And the hunters themselves now stalk seal and walrus with high-powered rifles and Japanese outboard motors.
Photographer:
Vladimir Vyatkin, USSR

● *Above*

Cadets at Moscow's Suvorov Military Academy brush their teeth at 07:15, after which they will make their beds at 07:38, pass inspection at 07:45 and complete their early morning routine with breakfast at 07:50.
Photographer:
Rick Smolan, USA

● *Following page*

Morning at the collective farm: In a scene right out of a Breughel painting, a crew of *traktoristi* (tractor drivers) enjoy a late breakfast in the fields after a morning of work near Kazan, in central Russia. Collective farms average 15,000 acres, often making travel from field to home quite a commute.
Photographer:
Bernd-Horst Sefzik, East Germany

A family sits down to breakfast
in their Khabarovsk apartment.
While most Soviet workplaces
have a *stolovaya* (cafeteria),
many people prefer to eat
breakfast and dinner at home.
Photographer:
Dilip Mehta, Canada

● *Left*

Omar Mamulashvili, 75, and his wife Nazi, 69, preside over an abundant family breakfast in the Georgian village of Dzalisi, near Tbilisi. The spread includes local specialities such as *khachapuri* (bread made with goat cheese), shashlyk (marinated skewered lamb), *tkemali* (sour plum sauce) and *lobio* (bean salad), as well as the ubiquitous Soviet cucumber.

Renowned for their hospitality, Georgians are frequent feasters. While trying to record family life in the Georgian countryside, American photographer Stephanie Maze lost many hours (and gained several pounds) at elaborate banquets held in her honor.
Photographer:
Stephanie Maze, USA

● *Above*

After a hearty breakfast of boiled carp with sour cream and *kumys* (fermented mare's milk), photographer Jay Dickman set out to see what he could photograph in Poltava, the Ukraine. He spotted this young girl wearing the red kerchief of a Young Pioneer walking to school with her mother.
Photographer:
Jay Dickman, USA

● *Left, above*

The Komi people of the Far
North have always relied on
roaming reindeer herds for food
and transportation. Though the
herds were decimated by a Soviet
attempt to organize collective
reindeer farms in the 1930s, their
numbers have since rebounded
to approximately 1.5 million
head. The Komi are now permitted to migrate across the tundra
with the herds, though the processing and distribution of
reindeer meat is still state run.
Photographer:
Sergei Samokhin, USSR

● *Left*

The day begins quietly as an
elektrichka from Zagorsk races
into Moscow. So called because
they run on electric power,
suburban commuter trains
belong to the working class.
High-ranking bureaucrats prefer
the private cars, either owner-
driven or chauffeured, which are
their privilege.
Photographer:
Ivan Sirota, USSR

● *Above*

A *babushka* brigade goes to
work on Tbilisi's streets. In a
society where women outnumber
men (especially among the older
generation devastated by World
War II), women play a primary
role in the workforce. Over 80
percent of females are employed, and it is not uncommon
to see women spreading asphalt
on roads, painting walls, working in rail yards and engaging in
other forms of manual labor.
Photographer:
Stephanie Maze, USA

● *Above*

Outside Yaroslavl Station,
Moscow.
Photographer:
Paul Chesley, USA

● *Right*

In a scene played out in hundreds of Soviet train stations
every spring and autumn, Kaliningrad families see their sons off
to the army. It is an old Russian
tradition to mark departure into
the army with a night of drinking and partying, and in rural
areas, entire villages often join
in the send-off. Like 80 percent
of all Soviet 18-year-olds, these
shaven *prizyvniki,* or conscripts,
undertake a grueling 2-year
training program with little
home leave or salary. The state
policy of mixing different Soviet
nationalities in each unit means
that these residents of the Soviet
Union's westernmost city could
end up as far away as Vladivostok, over 6,000 miles from
home.
Photographer:
Jan Tikhonov, USSR

● *Left*

A baker's dozen in Saratov: A nurse rolls in a fresh batch of infants from the maternity ward of Saratov's Emergency Hospital. Over 14,700 Soviet babies are born each day, and they come in more than a hundred varieties, including Byelorussian, Buryat, Bashkir, Chukchi, Chechen, Chuvash, Kazakh, Korean, Kalmyk, Tatar, Tajik, Tuvinian, Ukrainian, Uzbek, Udmurt and of course Russian—to name just a few.

Photographer:

Vladimir Lagranzh, USSR

● *Above*

Buns in the oven in Astrakhan: The Soviet Union produced 191,674,000 tons of grain in 1985, which went into *chyorny khleb, bulochki, rzhanoi khleb, kulich, mchadi, non, kalach, lavash, khachapuri, lekah, agnautka, polyanitsa, ukrainka, balabushki, korzh* and countless other regional recipes for that Soviet staple, bread.

Photographer:

Claus C. Meyer, West Germany

● *Above*

He's a 73-year-old veteran of The Great Patriotic War (World War II), proud of his physique and proud of his role in the defense of the Motherland. The swimming pool is at a new veterans hospital in suburban Kiev. Convalescent homes and other special facilities for the elderly are rarely necessary in the Soviet Union, where most retired people are cared for by their families. The exception is institutional care for needy war veterans, who hold a revered place in Soviet society.
Photographer:
Mary Ellen Mark, USA

● *Right*

Attending to weighty matters on an Odessa street corner. If you don't mind an audience, you can check your weight for just a few kopecks at public scales throughout the Soviet Union. Scale tenders, like coat checkers, door guards and other service people, are often retirees supplementing their state pensions.
Photographer:
Andy Levin, USA

● *Above*

Khava Soltakhanova brings back a bunch of spring onions from a "labor lesson" in Chechen Aul village, outside of Grozny. As part of their studies, all ninth- and tenth-graders living in the countryside learn how to work on a farm. The curriculum covers everything from milking cows to repairing combine harvesters.
Photographer:
Gerrit Fokkema, Australia

● *Right*

During phys ed class in Novo-voronezh, a young girl sizes up her prey during a game of *gorelki* or tag. Other Russian childhood games include *loshadi i vsadniki* (horses and riders) and *kazaki-razboiniki* (Cossacks and robbers).
Photographer:
Rudolf Frey, Austria

● *Following page*

Under the flags of the USSR and the Soviet Republic of Byelorussia, Minsk school children start their day with calisthenics.
Photographer:
Yuri Ivanov, USSR

Yuri Ivanov

Preschoolers at Khabarovsk's Kindergarten #188 rehearse for a pageant under the watchful eyes of "Uncle Lenin." From the time they enter school, Soviet children are taught to revere the founder of their nation. As one children's song puts it, "Lenin's life is an example to all people." Throughout the Soviet Union, Lenin's word is invoked in almost every conceivable situation. Depending on the context, however, his image passes through many subtle transformations. Here, an avuncular Lenin smiles with appropriate benevolence, while in nearly every Soviet public square, his bronze alter egos are stern and eternally vigilant.
Photographer:
Dilip Mehta, Canada

Order in the court: Chairman V.I. Terebilov and the Justices of the Supreme Court of the Soviet Union sit for American portrait photographer Neal Slavin. Unlike their American counterparts, the judges of the USSR's highest legal body do not hand down binding legal precedents, but provide lower courts with "guiding explanations" on how to interpret the Soviet legal code.
Photographer:
Neal Slavin, USA

● *Above*

Still kicking: the Bermukha (Old Oak) Folk Ensemble performs a traditional Georgian rain dance on a Batumi beach. No one knows if such dances work; but this Black Sea resort does have the highest annual rainfall and the most luxuriant vegetation of any Soviet city. The youngest member of the Bermukha chorus line is a sprightly 80 years old.
Photographer:
Corneliu Mocanu, Rumania

● *Right*

Morning exercise in a Baku park.
Photographer:
George Steinmetz, USA

For the cadets of Moscow's Suvorov Military Academy and Leningrad's Nakhimov Naval Academy, the road to command begins at age 15. Schooled in the handling of firearms and subject to strict military discipline, the young men pictured here quickly learn to think of themselves as officers in the Soviet armed forces.

Upon arrival at the Academy, cadets have completed eight years of primary school. During the next two years they will take the customary high school subjects, in addition to military courses. At graduation, they will receive the same *attestat zrelosti* ("attestation of maturity") conferred upon every Soviet high school student.

Still, the Suvorov and Nakhimov graduate is on one of the Soviet Union's few career fast tracks. With his specialized training, he stands a good chance of acceptance at one of the USSR's 140 military colleges, including the prestigious Frunze Academy, where Suvorov alumni make up over 30 percent of the student body. Many will be regimental commanders by the time they are 30.

Founded in World War II, both academies were initially intended for war orphans and the children of veterans. Entrance is based on competitive examina-

● *Above*

An early morning gym class at Moscow's *Suvorovskoe Uchilishche*.
Photographer:
Rick Smolan, USA

● *Right*

Morning drill at Nakhimov Naval Academy in Leningrad.
Photographer:
David Hume Kennerly, USA

tion, although tradition still tends to favor the children of military officers.

The atmosphere at Nakhimov took American photographer David Hume Kennerly by surprise: "Why are these military schools off limits to foreign journalists? There was nothing here which was shocking or embarassing—like any military school in the world the boys were taught fighting skills along with the normal subjects...On the one hand we were being given a chance to see and photograph things no one had ever seen before—and at the same time you couldn't figure out why they had ever restricted journalists from these places."

● *Above*

A Nakhimov tradition: Nina Zharova presents cadet Andrei Filunteyev with a nautical birthday pie. Moments later, the school's baker-in-residence gave photographer David Hume Kennerly a similar treat to commemorate his visit to the academy.
Photographer:
David Hume Kennerly, USA

● *Right*

At Moscow's Suvorov Military Academy, this cadet is getting by with a little help from his friend.
Photographer:
Rick Smolan, USA

● *Right*

A navigation class. Most classes at the naval academy are taught by experienced officers. In addition to their military studies, cadets must pass the same courses taken by every Soviet high-school student. When they graduate, these *Nakhimovtsy* will know Pushkin, Shakespeare, a foreign language, history, astronomy and Marxism-Leninism.
Photographer:
David Hume Kennerly, USA

Dilip Mehta

Previous pages 44–45	● *Previous pages 46-47*	● *Previous page*	● *Left*	● *Above*
ad workers lay blacktop in the rtile "Black Earth" region of ntral Russia, near the city of ratov. This scene is very differ- t from the one described by e playwright Chekhov, who lted his way across Russia in a ringless carriage in 1890: Never in my life have I laid eyes such a road, such terrible ush, and a roadway so horri-e, so neglected." The Soviets n now proudly travel over a illion miles of hard-surfaced ad, though vast areas of the untry, especially in Siberia, main impassable during the ring thaw. *Photographer:* **ladimir Lagranzh, USSR**	In a Khabarovsk park a pedes-trian takes an early-morning stroll past the Soviet Union's most ubiquitous symbol. The hammer and sickle ripples on every flag, is minted on every coin and peers out of every cor-ner of life in the Soviet Union. *Photographer:* **Dilip Mehta, Canada**	Bleary-eyed passengers arrive in Nakhodka's Tikhookeanskaya (Pacific Ocean) Station after an overnight ride on the *Vostok* (Eastern) train from Khaba-rovsk. *Washington Post* photog-rapher Frank Johnston traveled two days by plane and train across the entire Soviet Union to make this photograph. When he finally arrived in Nakhodka, he found that he was 5,900 miles from Moscow and only 650 miles from Tokyo. *Photographer:* **Frank Johnston, USA**	At the edge of the Ferghana Valley in the mountains of Kirghizia, 61-year-old Turdy Adiev and his white goshawk hunt for the small game of spring. In winter, Adiev and his fellow hunters use golden eagles to hunt wolves. Hunting with birds of prey is an ancient and revered sport in Central Asia, southern Siberia and Mongolia, and holds a special place in the oral epics and folk traditions of the region. *Photographer:* **Frans Lanting, Netherlands**	A smoking samovar awaits the Umetaliyev family, who will soon begin preparations for a mid-day feast. Though labor-saving electric samovars have been available for years, many Soviet families still use the tradi-tional charcoal-burning models for special occasions. *Photographer:* **Dmitri Baltermants, USSR**

● *Previous page*

The morning sun illuminates
birch trees in the Altai foothills,
less than 300 miles from the
Chinese border. Over 50
varieties of birch are indigenous
to the Soviet Union, so the Russians have made it a national
symbol, incorporating the tree
into many of their legends and
folktales.
Photographer:
James Balog, USA

● *Left*

Major General Ivan Fomenkov,
commander of the Suvorov
Military Academy in Moscow,
waits for an answer in his
spacious office. Multiple-line
phones are rare in the Soviet
Union, so it is not uncommon to
see six or more telephones on
some desks. In fact, the status of
a Soviet official can often be
determined by counting his
phones.
Photographer:
Rick Smolan, USA

● *Above*

Svetlana Romanyutina and
Anya Grumova, both book-
keepers in Murmansk's Fishing
Center, discuss a friend's wedding. Most Soviet offices lack
computer terminals, photo-
copiers and other electronic
gadgets without which the
average American workplace
would collapse. When Polish
photographer Jan Morek
scouted this office on May 14th,
he was delighted to see that the
accounts were done on ancient
abacuses, but when he returned
on May 15th to shoot, they had
all been replaced with shiny new
adding machines.
Photographer:
Jan Morek, Poland

● *Above*

Thousands of automated bobbins loaded with cotton fiber hum at a fabric factory in Dushanbe, capital of the central Asian republic of Tajikistan.
Photographer:
Jim Richardson, USA

● *Right*

At the Minsk Fine-Cloth Combine, workers take their gripes right to the top. Combine director Viktor Arbuzov and head engineer Yakov Vishnevsky listen, explain and take notes. The type of unscheduled meeting pictured here is called a *letuchka*.

Since General Secretary Gorbachev came to power, directors and managers have been asked to increase contact with their workers. If workers complain and no action is taken, ministerial investigations may ensue. Workers can also publish their complaints in newspapers.
Photographer:
Yuri Ivanov, USSR

● *Below*

In Turkmenistan, the southern-
most republic of the USSR,
Turkmen women wrapped
against the 100°F desert sun
hand-plant tomatoes. The republic encompasses a desert as
big as California called Qara
Qum or "black sand." Agricul-
ture is possible thanks to the
485-mile Qara Qum irrigation
canal.
Photographer:
Sebastiao Salgado, Brazil

One year after the Chernobyl nuclear disaster, the Soviet Union, one of the world's truly oil-rich nations, remains committed to nuclear energy. The USSR's 50 nuclear power plants now provide only 11 percent of the nation's electricity, but 11 new plants are under construction.

On May 15th, Austrian photographer Rudolf Frey was invited to visit a nuclear power plant outside Voronezh which had been built in 1982. He toured the plant's safety facilities and the control room at the newest of its five reactors, where he spotted the three panic switches (secured with string and sealing wax) that will shut down the reactor core in an emergency. Frey was amazed that he could have "just reached down and turned the thing off."

Since Chernobyl, the Soviet Union has been stung by a worldwide uproar over the meltdown and has taken some long overdue steps to improve its nuclear facilities: Moscow has fired—and prosecuted—several officials at the Chernobyl plant; canceled the construction of two additional reactors at Chernobyl; equipped three reactors similar to the one at Chernobyl with more advanced safety systems; halted the planning and construction of additional graphite-moderated reactors; and agreed in principle to the inspection of *some* Soviet plants by the International Atomic Energy Commission. In the meantime, Soviet propaganda continues to play down the dangers of nuclear energy. In May 1987, people listening to the English-language version of Radio Moscow's World Service were amused to hear that one year after the meltdown, the Chernobyl area was "fraught with no danger."

Photographer:
Rudolf Frey, Austria

Caviar (from the Turkish word *khavyah*—the Russians call it *ikra*) originates off the Caspian shorelines of Iran and the USSR. More precisely, it comes from the belly of the sluggish sturgeon who swim in these waters.

The Soviet caviar center of Astrakhan is ideally located on the mouth of the Volga River, where many sturgeon spawn. A single egg, measuring only one-tenth of an inch, can produce specimens up to 28

feet long and weighing 3,000 pounds, which, in turn, can yield up to 200 pounds of roe.

Extracting caviar is a delicate painstaking process. The fish is hauled from the Volga and taken to processing plant, where a worker carefully removes the eggs from the egg sac. The fish itself will not be discarded, as sturgeon was regarded as a great Russian delicacy long before anyone figured out what to do with the eggs.

When the membrane that holds the roe together is removed, the caviar gains its familiar pearl-grey luster and fine grain. A lucky quality control inspector samples the contents of each container before shipping. By the time the 2-pound tins hit capitalist shores, they will sell for well over a thousand dollars apiece.
Photographer:
Claus C. Meyer, West Germany

Called Siberia's Blue Pearl, Lake Baikal is a mile-deep canyon 400 miles long, containing 20 percent of the world's fresh water—more than all the Great Lakes combined. Three hundred and thirty-six rivers flow into Lake Baikal. It is home to over 2,000 species of flora and fauna, including the world's only freshwater seal and the *yepishura,* a tiny crustacean that devours decaying organic matter, and gives the icy azure lake its crystalline glitter.

Located in an area of tremendous economic importance, Lake Baikal was the focus of intensive industrial development for many years. Paper and lumber mills and a giant cellulose plant regularly dumped chemicals and untreated wood by-products into the lake.

In the early 1970s, a group of writers and scientists took up the Baikal cause and began to publicize its pollution problems. After years of protest, Moscow began to pay attention. A state-of-the-art water treatment station was installed near the pulp plant. Plans to divert several rivers flowing into Baikal were terminated, and the lake itself was declared a nature preserve.

Today, as the USSR becomes more aware of the dangers of pollution and the benefits of preserving wilderness, Lake Baikal is being promoted as a Soviet success story.

Photographer
Galen Rowell, USA

● *Above and right*

With the help of laser technology, Dr. Svyatoslav Fyoderov's "eye assembly line" can alleviate and even eliminate myopia. Professor Fyoderov's Institute of Eye Microsurgery leads the world in advanced eye surgery, and its methods are now used extensively in the West. Because of the Institute's international success, it has been given extraordinary privileges, including access to the best imported equipment. Financially accountable only to itself, the Institute's administrators use high salaries to lure some of the best medical minds in the Soviet Union. One of Fyoderov's nurses earns as much as a physician at an average Soviet hospital.

Photographer:
Viktor Chernov, USSR

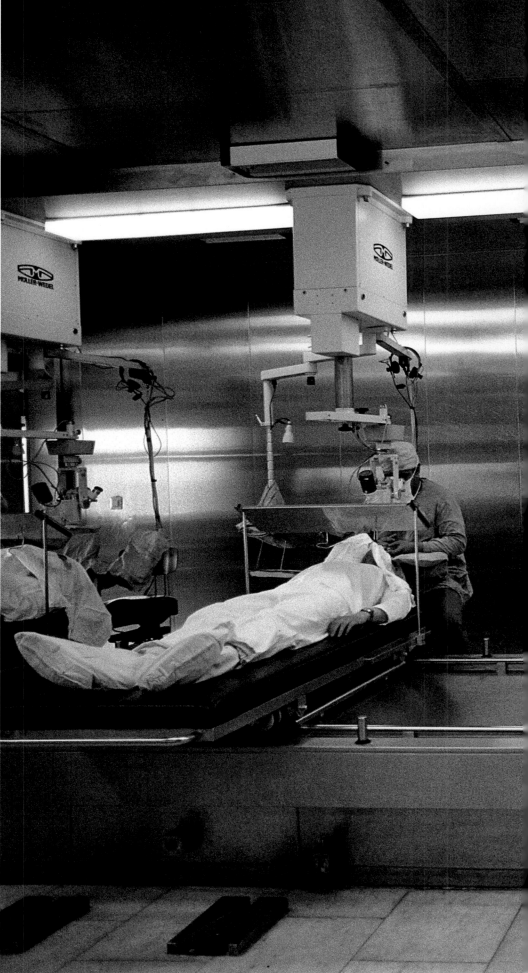

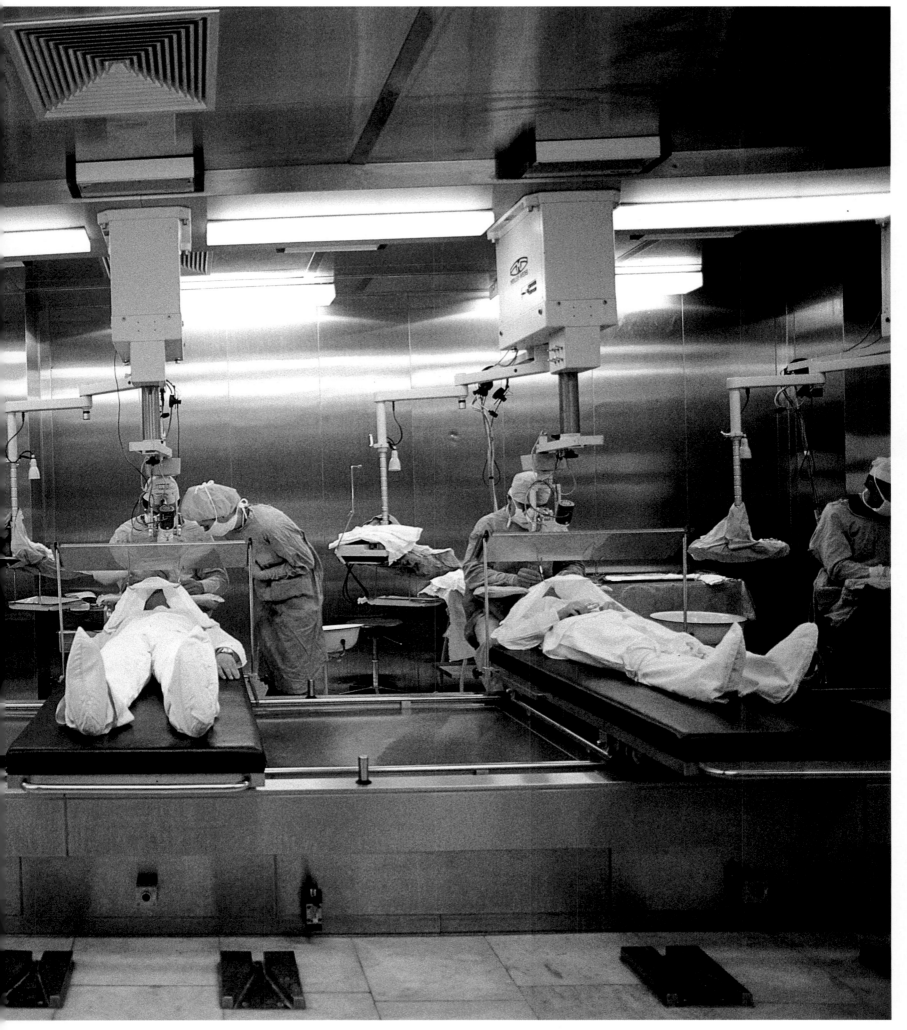

On May 15th, American photographer Mary Ellen Mark spent part of her day at the Kiev Special School for Blind Children #5.

Mark, who has done picture essays in America on children with cancer, retarded children and deaf children, was particularly impressed by the level of care she found in Kiev. "The aim of the school is to make the children completely self-sufficient. It was great to see how these kids who can't see live an essentially normal life. The reaction of the kids to me was great, too. It's amazing how everyone knows what a camera is. A lot of kids have been blind since birth, but everyone knew I was there from the shadow I threw. It was one of the most positive experiences I've ever had as a photographer."

Photographer:
Mary Ellen Mark, USA

● *Following page*

Grigori Chigogidze conducts a film class for Young Pioneers in Tbilisi, Georgia. The vast majority of 10-to 14-year-old Soviet children join the Pioneers. According to the solemn initiation oath, "A Pioneer is loyal to his Motherland, the Party and Communism. A Pioneer remembers the fallen fighters and prepares to be a defender of the Motherland."

Most of the time, however, a spirit of fun predominates.

Young Pioneers can learn about everything from astronomy to filmmaking at neighborhood "Pioneer Palaces." They are also entitled to wear the organization's traditional red kerchief. Its three corners represent the unity of the Pioneers, the Komsomol (Communist Youth League) and the final link in this civic *troika,* the Communist Party itself.

Photographer:
Stephanie Maze, USA

Nothing is a cliché to children. They see everything as if they were seeing it for the first time. Kodak supplied 100 Soviet schoolchildren with Kodak EF 35 mm cameras for use on May 15th. In return for their participation in *A Day in the Life of the Soviet Union,* the children were allowed to keep the cameras. Here is a selection from the 3,096 photos taken by this team of young photographers.

Timur Kamazov, Age 11   **Moscow**

Dima Malazhev, Age 10   **Moscow**

Sergei Popov, Age 12   **Kazym**

Sergei Ivanov, Age 12   **Moscow**

Denis Gankin, Age 11   **Moscow**

Igor Yashnov, Age 13   **Moscow**

Sergei Lebeder, Age 13 **Moscow**

Aleksei Vikterov, Age 13 **Bykovo**

Maksim Shenker, Age 10 **Moscow**

Igor Maltsev, Age 14 **Krasnoyarsk**

Roman Lavrik, Age 12 **Dickson**

Denis Skvortsov, Age 13 **Moscow**

Above

Bearing straight: An Eskimo
hunter keeps a steady course off
the mountainous coast of the
Chukotsk Peninsula, the Soviet
Union's easternmost point.
Photographer:
Vladimir Vyatkin, USSR

Above

Steady aim: Anatoli Konikhin
and Valeri Skhauche watch for
seal and walrus in the Bering
Sea. While Soviet Eskimos have
been modernized in many ways,
they still hunt for survival rather
than profit. Even that is a challenge in this rough, changeable
climate—halfway through the
hunt, a strong north wind began
to blow and snow flurries
obscured visibility for both
hunter and photographer.
Photographer:
Vladimir Vyatkin, USSR

● *Previous page*

Chewing the fat: Inside a small fabric-covered *balok,* or mobile cabin, Gennadi Porotov and Ignat Uksusnikov share a frozen fish and some private humor. The mask-like tans of the two Nganasan hunters come from long hours in the sun, wind and glaring snow.
Photographer:
Aleksandr Polyakov, USSR

● *Left*

Two motorcyclists scuffle with the law after disrupting an outdoor concert rehearsal in Votkinsk near Ustinov. Errant youths and juvenile delinquents, broadly called *khuligany,* or hooligans, are a frequent source of trouble for Soviet authorities. Acts of hooliganism, defined in the legal code as "intentional actions which grossly violate public order and express an obvious disrespect for society," account for 24 percent of all court convictions.
Photographer:
Gennadi Koposov, USSR

● *Above*

Two heavyweights (a lieutenant colonel and a captain) with the G.A.I., or traffic police, receive a report of trouble in central Moscow. More autonomous than their Western counterparts, Soviet traffic cops normally make on-the-spot decisions about who is at fault in a traffic accident, and then ask the guilty party to sign a sworn statement. All motorists carry traffic cards on which infractions and accidents are noted. When an officer cites a driver, he punches a hole in the card. Three punches and the driver starts using public transportation.
Photographer:
Torin Boyd, USA

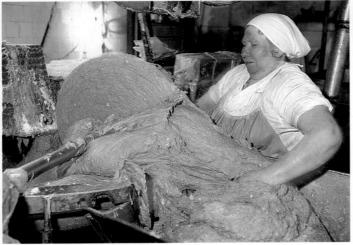

● *Above, top*

These little piggies went to
Tsentralny rynok, one of
Moscow's dozen or so open
markets. The variety and quan-
tity of produce at these empor-
iums contrasts markedly with the
limited selection found at the
average state-run store. As a
necessary concession to small
scale free enterprise, peasants
working at collective farms are
allowed to cultivate their own
small plots and sell the produce
at market price. Private plots
make up only 3 percent of the
Soviet Union's farm land, but
account for over 25 percent of
the nation's agricultural output.
Photographer:
Sarah Leen, USA

● *Above*

The daily grind: A woman
kneads sausage filling at a
Yakutsk meat plant. Pork and
beef is processed here, as well
as a local Yakut delicacy, wild
pony meat.
Photographer:
Diego Goldberg, Argentina

Relief workers distribute bread and milk to villagers from Smolino in Kurgan province. The Tobol River, swollen with heavy spring rains, had overflowed its banks, forcing many residents to leave their homes. When Hungarian photographer Lajos Weber arrived on the scene in an amphibious vehicle supplied by the local militia, the water had risen nearly 27 feet, and the army was struggling to keep the area supplied with food and clothing.
Photographer:
Lajos Weber, Hungary

● *Left*

Latif Karimov, an 82-year-old Azerbaijani master rug designer, sits in front of one of his creations: a rug in memory of V.I. Lenin. The banner behind Lenin proclaims, "Peace to all peoples." Azerbaijanis have been weaving carpets in the Persian tradition for centuries; however, the use of human figures in the design is a Soviet innovation.
Photographer:
George Steinmetz, USA

● *Above*

At a traditional handicrafts factory in the Ukrainian village of Reshetilovka, women slowly weave a carpet on a massive handloom. On May 15, 1987, workers were busy on a series of rugs commemorating the 70th anniversary of the Great October Revolution.
Photographer:
Jay Dickman, USA

● *Above*

On the line: An air force soldier uses a payphone in Astrakhan, a city on the Caspian Sea. Calls cost two kopecks (about three cents).
Photographer:
Claus C. Meyer, West Germany

● *Right*

In formation: A nurses' emergency brigade in Gorno Altaisk marches and sings patriotic songs before practicing procedures for large-scale civil emergencies such as epidemics, earthquakes, floods and wars.
Photographer:
James Balog, USA

● *Above, top*

Kindergarten children learn the mechanics of subtraction with the help of an abacus in Khiva, Uzbekistan. Although these youngsters begin school in their native Uzbek, they must eventually learn Russian to go on to higher education.

This fact irks some older non-Russians across the Soviet Union who worry about losing their native languages and culture. However, there are areas that have effectively managed to resist this cultural erosion, most notably Armenia, Georgia and the republics of Central Asia. In these regions with relatively few Russian immigrants, national languages are still dominant, forcing local Russian-speakers to become bilingual themselves.
Photographer:
Andrew Stawicki, Canada

● *Above*

A native-language school in the Siberian city of Yakutsk.
Photographer:
Diego Goldberg, Argentina

A Poltava kindergartener is temporarily banished to the hall for a minor breach of classroom etiquette. Many Soviet classrooms have a system of self-discipline in which one child, known as the *zvenovoi,* or group-leader, reports on the conduct of the other children in his or her row. Another scheme, known as *shefstvo,* assigns the best students to help weaker students with their schoolwork and general attitude.

In real life, these institutionalized systems don't always work. Older children roundly dislike their *zvenovye* and sometimes rough them up for tattling, while model students are accorded the same treatment by their peers as teachers' pets anywhere in the world.
Photographer:
Jay Dickman, USA

● *Left*

A waiter at Yerevan's Hotel Armenia tempts customers with two bottles of *Pepsi-Kola*. America's second-favorite soft drink has been number one in the USSR since 1959, when General Secretary Nikita Khrushchev took the Pepsi Challenge at an American trade fair in Moscow. Though Khrushchev fell from favor, Pepsi is still sold—lukewarm— at sidewalk kiosks in major Soviet cities.
Photographer:
Jodi Cobb, USA

● *Above*

Never say Neva: A young man balances his child on the banks of Leningrad's main waterway.
Photographer:
Nicole Bengiveno, USA

● *Above*

Sure cure: Vasili Shchetinnikov traveled over 1,000 miles from Omutninsk in northern Russia to take the cure at Matsesta near Sochi. His ailment: poor circulation in his extremities; his cure: the mineral-laden spring waters that bubble up at the ancient spa.

Photographer:

Aaron Chang, USA

● *Right*

Tots on pots: Preschoolers are communally toilet trained at the day-care center of a wood-finishing plant in the Buryat region. The children have their own numbered pots.

Photographer:

Seny Norasingh, USA

Dr. Vera Pazova of Gynecological Hospital #1 in Alma Ata presents the newborn daughter of local schoolteacher Liuda Andreyeva. Women comprise 70 percent of the USSR's medical doctors, a fact that has to do with low doctors' pay and the traditional notion that the caring professions are the domain of women.
Photographer:
Jean-Pierre Laffont, France

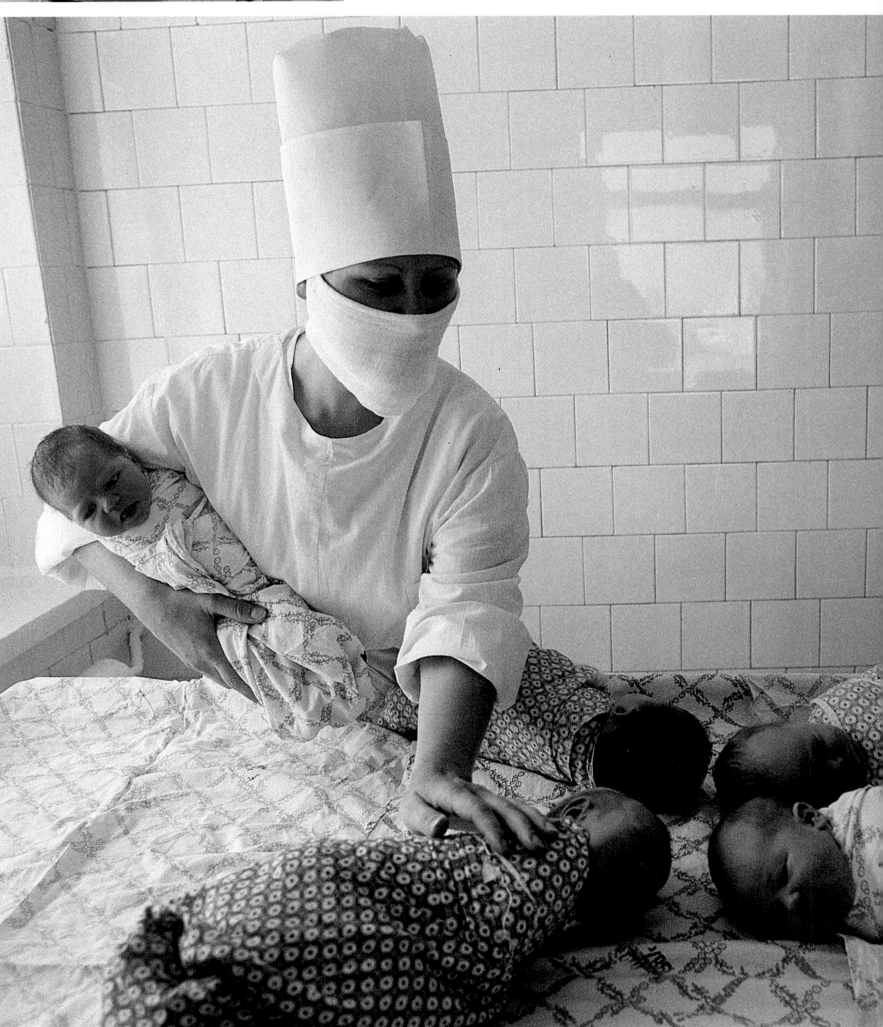

● *Left*

At the maternity hospital in Shevchenko, Kazakhstan, children's nurse Antonina Zadorozhkaya completes the swaddling of newborn infants. While the Russian population grew approximately 6 percent during the years 1970-79, the peoples of Central Asia, where the tradition of large families persists, increased their numbers by 25 percent.

Photographer:
Anatoli Morkovkin, USSR

● *Above, top*

It's a carriage! It's a sleigh! It's . . . Super Baby! It would take a super baby indeed to withstand the frigid temperatures of Dickson, located on the Soviet Union's Arctic shore. The mercury dips so low that parents have to take their children to school in these enclosed sleigh-carriages. It is the warmer weather, however, that they dread. When the snow melts, the ground becomes an impassable quagmire of mud.

Photographer:
Pavel Krivtsov, USSR

● *Above*

Baby boom: During rush hour, parking outside the kindergarten in Dickson can sometimes be a problem.

Photographer:
Pavel Krivtsov, USSR

● *Above*

On a roll: Streaking down a
Leningrad street on his-and-her
skateboards.
Photographer:
David Hume Kennerly, USA

● *Right*

Horsing around in Poltava:
Nikolai Zazulya makes his move
in mid-gallop while Anzhela
Khalimova tries to slow the
pace. "Kiss-a-girl" is played in
traditional Ukrainian costume
during festivals. The ostensible
goal is to sharpen riding skills.
Photographer:
Jay Dickman, USA

The bride takes the floor at a traditional Chechen wedding in a village near Grozny. The single men stay on one side of the room and the women on the other while the bride presides over the festivities, which usually last for three days. The groom sits out the entire ceremony—he only appears at the end to collect his new wife.

Photographer:
Gerrit Fokkema, Australia

Eternal flames: A young groom takes his bride to a World War II memorial in Tallin. Since the average wedding ceremony takes only a few minutes, many Soviet couples spend their first day as husband and wife touring the landmarks of their hometown in a rented *Chaika* limousine. A stop at the local war memorial is *de rigueur.*

Photographer:
Raphaël Gaillarde, France

At the altar in Alma Ata: Tolegen Shynybayev kisses the hand of his new bride, Tynyshtyq, during their wedding ceremony at the *Neke Saraiy*, or Wedding Palace. The bride is wearing a traditional Kazakh wedding dress.

Photographer:
Jean-Pierre Laffont, France

● *Above*

Aleksei Sorubnev leaves the Norilsk Wedding Palace with his new wife, Yelena Fedorova. Like many other remote Siberian industrial towns, Norilsk offers high salaries and rapid advancement to anyone willing to brave the cold. Since the takers tend to be ambitious college graduates with no family ties, Norilsk has become a fertile meeting ground for young lovers.
Photographer:
Vladimir Fedorenko, USSR

● *Following page*

Waiting for the big moment: A Khabarovsk couple waits their turn at the local Palace of Weddings, which handles as many as 40 ceremonies a day. For a small fee, couples can stay for champagne and chocolates after the seven-minute ceremony, but most proceed directly to their own more elaborate celebrations.
Photographer:
Dilip Mehta, Canada

● *Above, top*

Vladimir Slepak, 58, and his wife, Mariya, 60, are "refuseniks," Jews who have been denied emigration visas by the state. Despite a policy that allows emigration when a significant number of family members reside outside the country (Mariya Slepak's mother, sister and son are in Israel and another son is in New York), the Slepaks have been refused exit visas for nearly two decades.

Since Vladimir Slepak first applied to leave the USSR in 1970, he has been constantly harassed, tailed and searched, interrogated at least 20 times, fired from 5 jobs (from radio engineer to watchman), exiled to Siberia for 5 years and put in detention twice. The stubborn courage of the Slepaks has made them the best-known Soviet refuseniks in the world.

Photographer:
Gary Eisenberg, USA

● *Above*

"Stop Alcohol Production": Concerned citizens protest against drinking—a national pastime. The Soviets have traditionally consumed staggering amounts of vodka (4 gallons a year for every man, woman and child), drinking even their nearest rivals (the Poles at 1.4 gallons) under the statistical table. Alcoholism is blamed for most of the crimes (including 90 percent of murders), two-thirds of all work-related accidents and half of all divorces in the Soviet Union. General Secretary Gorbachev has replaced the half-hearted anti-drinking policies of his predecessors with strong anti-alcohol measures, including severe cutbacks in the number of places and hours where and when alcohol can be sold. This apparent protest march, for example, is probably government sponsored.

Photographer:
Aleksandr Tombulidis, USSR

"Let there always be sky," says one placard; "Let there always be sun," says another. The placards are being brandished by members of a women's peace march moving down one of Khabarovsk's unusually wide avenues. The ever-fervent, government-sponsored Soviet Committee for Defense of Peace coordinates "peace days, friendship months" and "disarmament weeks" throughout the country and cooperates with international peace organizations.
Photographer:
Dilip Mehta, Canada

● *Left*

Customers crowd the footwear section of Moscow's State Department Store, the Soviet Union's largest. *GUM* (pronounced "goom") was built between 1889 and 1893. The long glass-roofed shopping arcades are still intact, even if the present selection of merchandise seems slightly out of place in the midst of all the fin-de-siècle splendor. Photographer Rick Smolan chanced upon a rare desirable shipment of imported shoes, and was astonished to see that, no matter what the style, if the shoe fit, or came close to fitting, the customer bought a pair immediately.
Photographer:
Rick Smolan, USA

● *Above*

An elderly couple shops for seafood in Nakhodka's huge Okean Fish Store. Because Nakhodka houses one of the largest Soviet fishing fleets in the Far East, this supermarket is unusually well stocked with fresh fish and marine delicacies such as crab legs. The city's port, constructed in 1950, is also home to the only joint Soviet-American company in existence, the US-USSR Marine Resources Co.
Photographer:
Frank Johnston, USA

Yerevan, Armenian SSR

Jodi Cobb, USA

Makhachkala, RSFSR

Janusz Fogler, Poland

Khanty Mansiisk, RSFSR

Yuri Kaver, USSR

Yalta, Ukrainian SSR

Arthur Grace, US

Zagorsk, RSFSR   Tomasz Tomaszewski, Poland   Moscow, RSFSR   Paul Chesley, USA

tim, RSFSR   Boris Babanov, USSR

● *Left*

On Kikhnu Island, two and one-half hours by boat from Estonia, these women share a motorcycle ride to market. Isolation from the mainland has helped the 500 islanders, two-thirds of whom are female, to preserve their traditions.

Photographer:
Yuri Vendelin, USSR

● *Above*

Though his horse doesn't seem too impressed, ace shepherd Taspalad Akhmatov of the village of Gani Bazar in Kirghizstan has won three Orders of Lenin and the Order of the October Revolution for outstanding achievement in the workplace—in this case, the summer pasturelands in the foothills of the Tien Shan Mountains.

Photographer:
Frans Lanting, Netherlands

● *Below*

Heavily decorated show collies Antosha, Amikus and Kazha show off in Babushkin, a Moscow suburb. The growth of disposable income has fueled an explosion in the number of household pets in the USSR.

Photographer:

Torin Boyd, USA

● *Below, middle*

In Kazakhstan, on the Aksuatsky State Farm, a young irascible camel suffers the indignities of simultaneous milking and shearing. *Shchuvak,* or camel's milk, is considered more desirable than cow's milk; in Moscow, it is a gourmet item.

Photographer:

Aleksandr Sentsov, USSR

● *Left, bottom*

Grin and bear it: Trainer Lyuba Kudryatseva supervises an ursine hair-styling backstage at the Sochi Circus. Like many Soviet circus performers, Kudryatseva graduated from a special circus school in Kiev and started her career as an acrobat before marrying celebrated bear trainer Nikolai Kudryatsev.

Photographer:

Aaron Chang, USA

● *Below*

Veterinarian Sergei Yemelyanov makes his morning rounds on Poltava's Dubrovka Horse Farm. This 250-acre Ukrainian farm breeds racehorses, some of which trace their bloodlines back to the American champion, Low Hanover, which the Soviets purchased in the 1950s. On the morning of May 15th, only one of the farm's 700 horses was feeling slightly indisposed.

Photographer:

Jay Dickman, USA

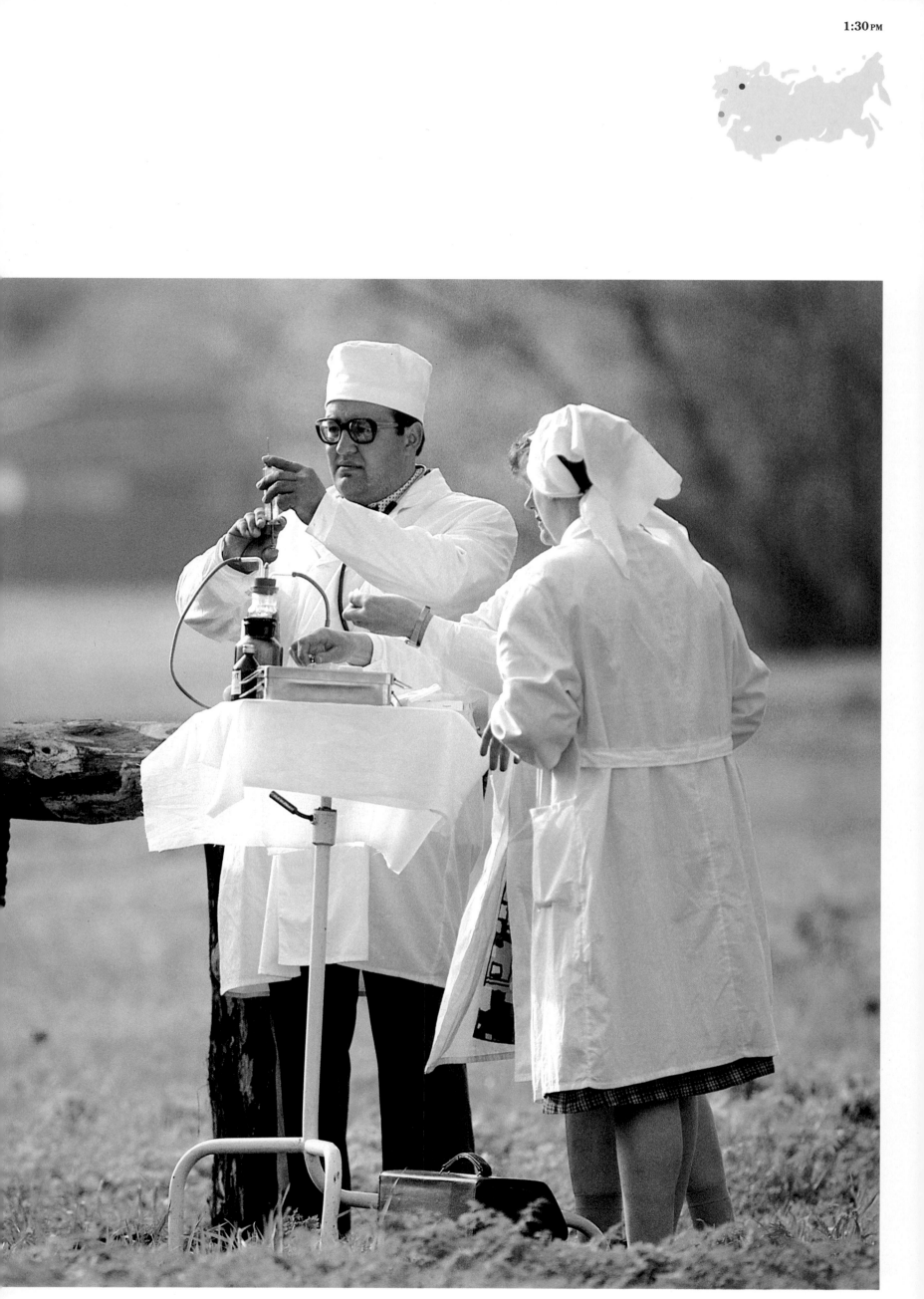

● *Below*

Sheep graze in the foothills of the Tien Shan Mountains in Kazakhstan. The Kazakh shepherd is carrying on the work that has occupied his nomadic people for centuries, though now he works under the auspices of the *Souanbai kolkhoz* (collective farm). Beyond the snowy Tien Shan peaks lies the People's Republic of China.

Photographer:

Jean-Pierre Laffont, France

Before her death in 1972, Alla Tarasova was a leading actress in the Moscow Art Theater and a model Communist Party leader. Her funeral might normally have received wide press coverage in the Soviet Union, but it was never publicized. Tarasova had requested a Christian burial, so local authorities—members of the officially atheistic Communist Party—cold-shouldered the funeral.

Tarasova's case is an eloquent example of the uneasy and complicated relationship between church and state in the Soviet Union. Technically, the Soviet Constitution guarantees all citizens the right to "freedom of conscience, that is, the right to profess any religion. . .and to perform religious worship." The Communist Party, however, is doggedly committed to atheism.

The Party wants eventually to eradicate religious belief in the USSR, but in a society where 15 to 20 percent of the adult population, approximately 32 million people, declare themselves believers, this goal is not easily accomplished. Ramadan fasts and religious marriages are still widely observed by Moslems; Easter services in Moscow are so popular that volunteer police forces are necessary to control the crowds; baptism, recently described by the govern-

● *Above*

A 24-year-old Roman Catholic priest, the youngest in the USSR, hears confession at St. Albert's Church in Riga. In recent years, the Soviet government has fostered a relationship with the Vatican, a development that bodes well for the Baltic states and their thousands of Roman Catholic citizens.
Photographer:
Patrick Tehan, USA

● *Right*

In Echmiadzin, home of the Armenian Church, the faithful meet for prayer. An ancient form of Christianity, the Armenian Church dates from 301 A.D.
Photographer:
Oleg Makarov, USSR

● *Below*

Metropolitan Surozhski and
Metropolitan Pitirim, both high-
ranking bishops of the Russian
Orthodox Church, ride to an or-
dination ceremony in Moscow.
Photographer:
Ivan Sirota, USSR

ment journal *Science and Religion* as "primitive, superstitious and unhealthy," is on the increase.

Still, in this epic struggle for the hearts and minds of Russia, the rules, not surprisingly, favor state atheism. The nation's 9,000 churches, mosques and synagogues are all the property of the state. While the Constitution says worship is free, in practice, any attempt to spread religious belief is punished. Thus, Jews are technically free to go to services on Friday evening, but are not allowed to organize Hebrew classes. Members of proselytizing Protestant sects are fined and harassed. And only material espousing

● *Above, top*

At Moscow's Vagankovo Cemetery, mourners pay their last respects at a group funeral. Following the service, conducted according to Russian Orthodox liturgy, only family members will remain for the burial.
Photographer:
Nikolai Ignatiev, USSR

● *Above*

A woman lights a candle at the Nikolski Orthodox Church in Leningrad.
Photographer:
Nicole Bengiveno, USA

atheism can be distributed. (A well-financed network of clubs, museums and newspapers has been created to carry out this task.)

The largest and most powerful religious institution in the USSR is the Russian Orthodox Church. Bolstered by tens of millions of believers, it is the wealthiest private organization in the country, wielding tremendous power and influence. Though it has been brutally repressed in the past, the Church is now permitted to operate over two dozen convents and monasteries and over 7,500 churches. In return, Orthodox leaders occasionally act as spokesmen for the government, backing the Soviet claim that the state allows freedom of worship. The Church also makes generous donations to the Soviet Peace Committee and other state-sponsored causes.

This delicate balancing act has characterized church-state relations in the USSR since Brezhnev. Instead of harsh restrictions, authorities now regulate all religious activity through the Council for Religious Affairs, which has ministerial status. Other religious organizations, like the four Spiritual Directorates which govern the affairs of Soviet Islam, are manned by Moslem officials loyal to Moscow.

The Moslems present Soviet authorities with particular difficulties. In the intricate web of Soviet society, religion and nationality are often intertwined, and for Moslems, like the Armenian Orthodox and the Lithuanian Catholics, faith is a touchstone of national identity. Jews, too, are caught between religion and nationality. Traditional Russian anti-Semitism and government atheism campaigns have caused tens of thousands of Jews to deny or disguise their religious heritage. Worship is clandestine, and the synagogues of European Russia are frequented only by elderly men.

The photographs shown here are only a handful of

● *Above, top*

Lamaist Buddhist monks attend morning prayers at Ivolga Temple near Ulan Ude in Buriatia. Ethnically Mongolians, the Buriats converted to the Tibetan form of Buddhism in the 16th century. Ivolga Temple, funded by donations from the local faithful, was built in 1973.
Photographer:
Seny Norasingh, USA

● *Above*

Friday is the Moslem holy day. At the Khoja Abdu Darun Mosque in Samarkand, a group of Sunni Moslems mark the end of a *rakaat* (prayer) by drawing their hands down over their faces. The pure white turbans worn by the three men in the center of the picture signify that the wearers are scholars of the Koran, able to recite the holy work in the original Classical Arabic.
Photographer:
Gerd Ludwig, West Germany

● *Right*

At an uncrowded Friday evenin Sabbath service at the Tbilisi Synagogue, a man follows alor in his prayer book. More than of the 60 synagogues left in the Soviet Union are in the Georgia Republic.
Photographer:
Stephanie Maze, USA

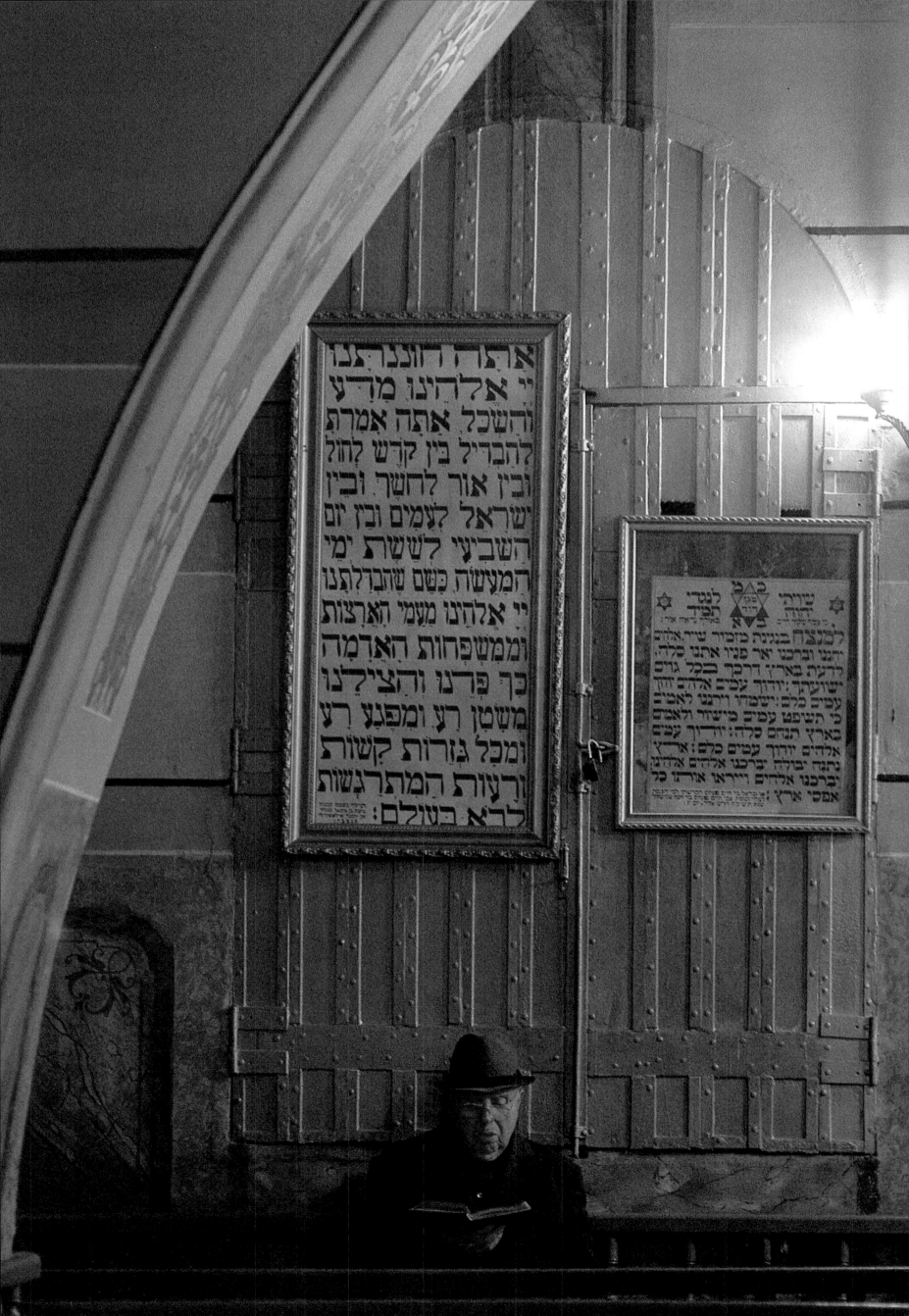

the thousands of powerful images of religious ritual and celebration taken on May 15th. It is worth noting that both the Orthodox Church and the Soviet press agency, Novosti, went out of their way to provide *Day in the Life* photographers with special access to religious subjects. The Church needs publicity in the West to support its cause, and the Soviets, in line with their international propaganda in this area, wanted to showcase their religious tolerance. Regardless, religious faith is alive and well in a nation often considered to be a godless society.

● *Left*

The cathedral at the Pyukhta Convent, one of 12 Russian Orthodox nunneries, seems to disappear into the misty Estonian morning.
Photographer:
Marina Yurchenko, USSR

● *Above*

Sister Nataliya of the Pyukhta Convent was formerly an art expert and Leningrad resident. She entered the convent nine years ago.
Photographer:
Marina Yurchenko, USSR

Diego Goldberg

● *Previous page*

Wild ponies are herded in the freshly fallen snow on a *sovkhoz* (state farm) near the city of Yakutsk. Small and stocky, these ponies are bred by the indigenous Yakuts for their ability to withstand winters that are frigid even by Siberian standards: average temperatures in January range from − 18°F to − 58°F.
Photographer:
Diego Goldberg, Argentina

● *Above*

General Secretary Mikhail Gorbachev leans on his desk as he and Foreign Minister Eduard Shevardnadze await the arrival of French Prime Minister Jacques Chirac. May 15th was a busy day for the General Secretary, who commutes from his home on the western outskirts of Moscow to his Kremlin office between 9 and 10 in the morning and stays until 8 p.m. Gorbachev's vigorous style takes him on the road more often than his predecessors, making him unusually visible for a Soviet leader. Private portraits are extremely rare, however, and veteran Soviet photographer Yuri Abramochkin was given only 90 seconds to capture this image.
Photographer:
Yuri Abramochkin, USSR

● *Right*

At the Yuri Gagarin Cosmonaut Training Center (named for the pioneering Soviet cosmonaut), Syrian spaceman Munir Habib and his Russian comrade, Anatoli Solovyov, practice simulated re-entry for an upcoming joint mission to the orbiting Soyuz-Mir space station. The training center, located less than 20 miles outside of Moscow in Zvyozdny Gorodok (Star City), prepares Soviet and foreign cosmonauts for space flights. The actual launches occur in Baikonur in a remote section of Kazakhstan.
Photographer:
Roger Ressmeyer, USA

● *Following page*

A neutral-buoyancy tank at Star City simulates weightlessness in space. Cosmonauts-in-training use the tank and a mock-up of a Mir space station to practice a zero-G rescue. A real Mir station has been orbiting the earth for over 15 months, setting another space-age record for the Soviets.
Photographer:
Roger Ressmeyer, USA

After a day on the assembly line, workers at Togliatti's Volga Automobile Works sample a taste of workers' paradise in the plant's relaxation room. Togliatti, the Motor City of the Soviet Union, was named after the co-founder of the Italian Communist Party. The auto works were built with the help of Fiat Motors; *la dolce vita* comes courtesy of the plant management.

Photographer:
Jerry Valente, USA

● *Left*

● *Above*

Children at Stavropol's School #26 catch their rays from a quartz lamp. Far from being a toddler tanning salon, this treatment has a medical purpose: it is believed to prevent vitamin D deficiency. Stavropol, General Secretary Gorbachev's hometown, is not exactly starved for sunlight, but in far northern cities like Murmansk the sun doesn't rise for two months each winter. Goggles and a circle drawn on the floor insure that no one suffers an overdose.
Photographer:
Wally McNamee, USA

All the *glasnost* that's fit to print: Pedestrians on Gorki Street, one of Moscow's busiest thoroughfares, peruse the government daily *Izvestiya* on a newspaper billboard. Any one of a dozen periodicals, including *Krasnaya zvezda* (Red Star, the army newspaper), *Sovetsky sport* (Soviet Sport) and *Selskaya zhizn* (Rural Life) can be read by pedestrians on hundreds of billboards throughout the city. It used to be said that there was no *pravda* (truth) in *Izvestiya* and no *izvestiya* (news) in *Pravda,* but the press under Gorbachev has entered a period of unprecedented candor. Coverage of such hot (and formerly taboo) topics as Stalinism and the purges, industrial accidents like the Chernobyl nuclear disaster, large-scale corruption and youth problems are sending the circulation figures of leading urban dailies skyrocketing.
Photographer:
Yuri Abramochkin, USSR

● *Left*

These coin-operated *sok* (juice) machines near a Moscow school dispense a glassful of grape juice for 20 kopecks (about 31 cents). In general, vending machines in the USSR dispense soda water or juice, but no containers. Instead, the user must wash out the communal glass provided with each machine. Bringing your own glass is regarded as *nekulturny,* a word Russians apply to behavior that violates certain unspoken rules of etiquette.
Photographer:
Paul Chesley, USA

● *Above*

Each member of the "Fighting Friends," a club for female World War II veterans, has eight or more military decorations. During the massive mobilization of 1941-45, women were widely employed in the army and behind the lines. Their heroic exploits at the front and in the factories are recounted in popular wartime lore. After posing for a group portrait, Tamara Nikolayeva, 62, and Valentina Podomekina, 65, performed an impromptu Russian dance.
Photographer:
Fridrikh Grinberg, USSR

● *Left*

Soldiers at the Tamansky
Motorized Infantry Division
near Moscow show lots of
square-jawed spirit during a
field review.
Photographer:
D. Gorton, USA

● *Above*

Sub-freezing weather can't stop
the residents of Karataikha,
Siberia (population: 650) from
demonstrating their civic pride.
Photographer:
Boris Babanov, USSR

A young bodybuilder nick-named "Jail" (so-called because he prefers to work out alone) exhibits his sculpted physique in a basement gym in the working-class Moscow suburb of Lyubertsy. Young toughs from this section, called Lyubers, became notorious after a 1987 article in *Ogonyok* magazine depicted them as a gang of fear-some teenage vigilantes. According to *Ogonyok,* the Lyubers sometimes roam the streets of Moscow harassing hippies, punks, heavy-metal fanatics and other nonconformists.

According to the photographer, who prefers to remain anonymous, "I asked some well-built boys who the strongest Lyuber was, and they told me it was a man nick-named Jail. People were afraid to direct me to him. I was told that these Lyubers didn't like anything Western and might beat me up if I told them who I was shooting for. When I eventually found the basement gym, Jail's wife was crying outside because she thought he had taken a girl down there and spent the night with her. He had locked himself in the basement and wouldn't come out. I thought I wasn't going to be able to shoot anything until some friends took the wife away to comfort her and I sneaked in. Jail and his friends were working out and had no objections to me taking pictures. They were proud of their muscles, and looking forward to a body-building competition taking place in Lyubertsy next week."
Photographer:
Anonymous, USSR

On May 15th, Pulitzer Prize-winning photographer Eddie Adams went to Vladimir Prison, a medium-security facility about 150 miles east of Moscow. It was the first time any photojournalist had ever visited Vladimir, the former "Isolator" of Aleksandr Solzhenitsyn's, *The Gulag Archipelago.*

"When we arrived," Adams says, "I didn't even know we were at the prison because the buildings had been painted pink with green doors and blue trim."

Adams, who was allowed one 20-minute shooting session, soon found that every picture he wanted to take had to be approved by the warden. By the time he received permission, the subject had moved or disappeared and the picture was gone. After the shoot, Adams voiced his frustration. "I told them I thought they were stupid for not allowing me to shoot the pictures I wanted since the prison looked pretty good." After a long harangue, Adams finally convinced the officials to take him back to Vladimir.

"So, we went back to the prison. . .into a factory on the premises where the prisoners worked. It looked like something out of the Depression. I was only there for 5 minutes, if that. It was very dark; hardly any light whatever, and I was shooting like crazy. Finally, this seemed to be the real Vladimir."

● *Left*

After lunch (and some vigorous complaints from the photographer): Adams was admitted to the prison's machine shop where inmates were making doorknobs, wrenches and other tools.
Photographer:
Eddie Adams, USA

● *Above*

Before lunch: Photographer Eddie Adams was presented with this idyllic scene of inmates enjoying some recreational reading in Vladimir Prison's sunlit courtyard.
Photographer:
Eddie Adams, USA

● *Above*

Workers at Odessa's Ilyichevsk
Ship Repair Factory blast old
paint from the hull of a freighter
before applying a new finish.
Odessa is one of the Soviet
Union's most important ports.
Unlike northern Soviet coastal
cities, it remains ice-free for
most of the winter.
Photographer:
Andy Levin, USA

● *Right*

Net profits: A brigade of weavers
from the Kirov fishing kolkhoz
unwinds at the end of the working day in the village of Ozersk
on Sakhalin Island. This mountainous 29.5-thousand-square-
mile territory was a notorious
penal colony under the Tsars. In
1983, Korean Airlines flight 007
strayed over Sakhalin and was
shot out of the skies by Soviet
warplanes.
Photographer:
Igor Gavrilov, USSR

Kaliningrad, RSFSR   Jan Tikhonov, USSR

Moscow, RSFSR   Raphaël Gaillarde, France   Grozny, RSFSR   Gerrit Fokkema, Austral

Khabarovsk, RSFSR

Dilip Mehta, Canada

Narym, RSFSR

Sergei Edisherashvili, USSR

● *Above*

KRASNOYARSK! Exuberant signage enlivens a traffic circle and promotes civic pride in Krasnoyarsk, Siberia, population: 800,000.
Photographer:
Feliks Solovyov, USSR

● *Right*

For young workers frustrated by long waits for new apartments, there's an alternative: Build your own home. Do-it-yourselfers must find their own materials and provide the labor. The house plot itself is retained by the government, owner of every square inch of the Soviet Union and, as a result, the largest land-owner in the world.
Photographer:
Feliks Solovyov, USSR

Above

A motley assortment of *dachi*,
or country homes, climbs a
hillside outside Kazan in central
Russia. Residents pay a small tax
on the land where the house is
situated, but are otherwise free
to build on the plot as they wish.
Having a *dacha* — which can
mean anything from tin-roofed
cottages like these to spacious
pre-Revolutionary estates — is a
mark of privilege in a society
where housing is at a premium.
Photographer:
**Bernd-Horst Sefzik, East
Germany**

● *Above*

Uniform rows of housing line
Krasnaya Presnya Avenue in
Tynda. The pressure to provide
more living space is tremendous,
especially in booming industrial
centers like this one, and entire
neighborhoods are often completed before they can be supplied with adequate stores,
phone service and bus routes. In
1985 alone, approximately one
billion square feet of new housing were completed.
Photographer:
Viktor Rudko, USSR

● *Left*

Khabarovsk preschoolers on
the rooftop playground of
Kindergarten #188. The hair
bow is *de rigueur* for all Soviet
preschool girls.
Photographer:
Dilip Mehta, Canada

● *Above*

Little squirt Karim Shamsiyev
drinks from the tap at the
Rossiya Collective Farm outside
Dushanbe, capital of Tajikistan.
Photographer:
Jim Richardson, USA

● *Above*

Customers at a Leningrad hair salon wait for their hairstyles to dry. Like many Soviet women, the *blondinka* in the middle favors an elaborate perm.
Photographer:
Mark S. Wexler, USA

● *Right*

Women compare values at the Moda clothing store in Moscow. This crowd scene is a familiar one in the Soviet Union. Planning for the Soviet centralized economy has failed to provide sufficient consumer goods. The result is shortages, followed by a mad rush whenever a desired product appears in stock. Another problem is the near-byzantine intricacy of shopping in a Soviet store; to purchase a bra, for example, customers will line up three times — to make a selection, to pay for the purchase and finally to pick up the goods.
Photographer:
Sarah Leen, USA

A Leningrad customer receives a *pedikyur*.
Photographer:
Mark S. Wexler, USA

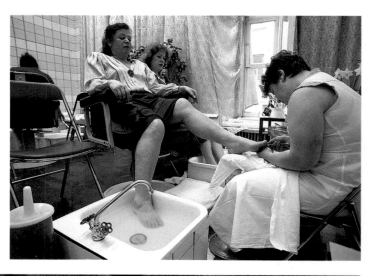

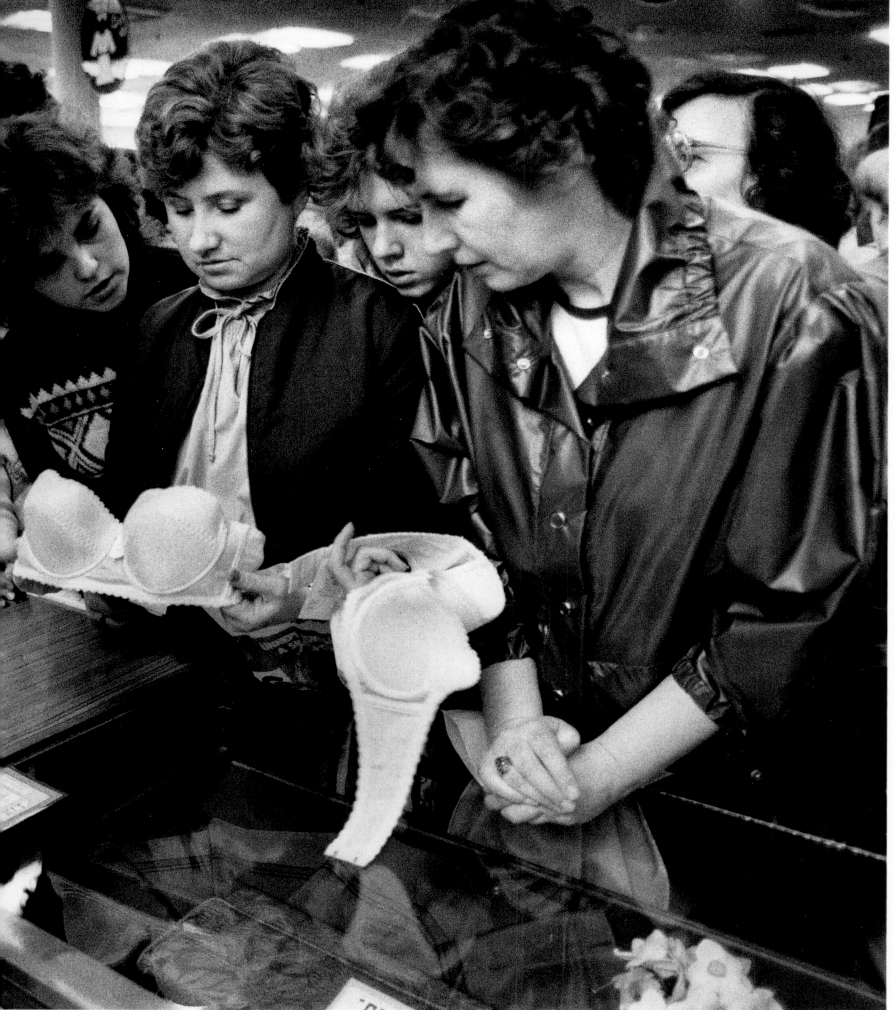

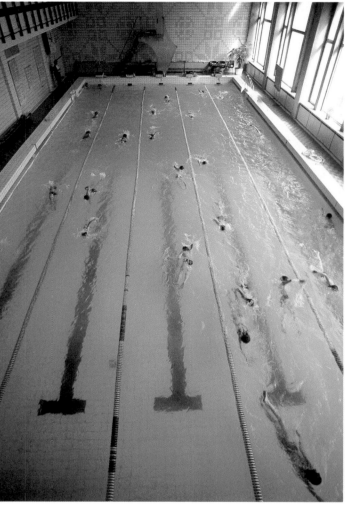

● *Left*

Tskhenburi practice near Sukhumi. Most towns in the region sponsor teams to play this ancient Persian form of polo.
Photographer:
Steve Krongard, USA

● *Above*

In Minsk, at the Palace of Culture and Sports, one of the Soviet Union's 2,500 swimming pools gets a good workout.
Photographer:
Pat Field, USA

● *Above*

Snow falls on the Arctic town of Dickson, temperature: − 22°F.

"The cold," a visitor to the Far North once wrote, "makes the newcomer aware of his nose for the first time; every hair inside freezes rigid in a second. You can actually feel them bending with each intake of breath. Naturally, you can see your breath, but what is more extraordinary, you can hear it turn to ice."

Photographer:
Pavel Krivtsov, USSR

● *Right*

On the plaza outside Lenin Stadium, a Moscow skateboard hangout, Vladimir Morozov cruises in the sunshine. The 19-year-old university student says he used to skateboard here with all his friends, but a lot of them are now in the army.

Photographer:
Torin Boyd, USA

● *Above*

Tossing lightweight balls into the
air helps elderly patients at the
Institute for Gerontology keep
their reflexes sharp. The Institute, located in Kiev, specializes
in the rehabilitation of patients
with Parkinson's disease and
carries out intensive research
into longevity and the aging
process.

Photographer:
Matthew Naythons, USA

● *Right*

The citizens of Leningrad endure eight months of cold
weather a year, so given the
chance, they are zealous sun-
worshippers. The beach-of-
choice for many city bathers is in
front of the Peter and Paul Fortress. Built by Peter the Great in
1703 on an island in the Neva
River, the Fortress served as
a pre-Revolutionary jail for
political prisoners.

Photographer:
David Hume Kennerly, USA

● *Above, top*

When the spring sun finally shines, a Volgograd park bench beckons. The head goes back, the shoes come off...
Photographer:
David C. Turnley, USA

● *Above*

These Yalta sunbathers seem oblivious to the seaside *remont* (the ubiquitous Russian word for the nearly constant repair work that goes on in the Soviet Union) taking place behind them. In February 1945, this Crimean resort hosted the most momentous beach party in history—the Yalta Conference, at which Stalin, Roosevelt and Churchill met to shape post-war Europe.
Photographer:
Arthur Grace, USA

Attendance was poor at the May 15th meeting of the Murmansk Walrus Club: Members complained that 33°F was far too warm for serious swimming. After their dip in the water, these "walruses" will jog home, wearing nothing but their swimsuits and sneakers.
Photographer:
Jan Morek, Poland

A sloppy spring blizzard hits downtown Norilsk in north-central Siberia.
Photographer:
Vladimir Fedorenko, USSR

● *Left*

Holding a ceremonial mask, a hunter pauses during the Bear Feast, a traditional Khanty festival in the village of Tiltim. For his assignment, Soviet photographer Boris Babanov joined an expedition set up by the Sverdlovsk Institute of the North to study the effects of modern civilization on the indigenous peoples of the North. The journey took him across hundreds of miles of taiga by helicopter and finally, on May 15th, to this small settlement in the northern Ural Mountains.
Photographer:
Boris Babanov, USSR

● *Above*

Parents pick up their children at a Yakutsk *detsky sad* (kindergarten). The state has increasingly assumed the role of the *babushka,* who would take care of the grandchildren while their parents were at work. In urban areas, where two-income families are the norm, up to three-quarters of all children spend their days in *yasli* (daycare centers for children three months to three years) and kindergartens. These children are tightly bundled against a chilly Siberian spring: even in winter, Yakutsk schools do not close unless the temperature dips below − 58°F.
Photographer:
Diego Goldberg, Argentina

● Above

Commuters disembark at Moscow's Yaroslavl Station, terminus for trains from the Far North, Beijing and Ulan Bator as well as nearby suburbs. The Trans-Siberian from Vladivostok pulls in here at 4:40 p.m. every day—usually right on schedule after seven full days of travel.
Photographer:
Paul Chesley, USA

● Right

Two Buryat schoolchildren ride the *tramvai* home in Ulan Ude, near the Mongolian border. Ulan Ude does not get very many foreign visitors, and *Day in the Life* photographer Seny Norasingh, now a US citizen but originally from Laos, was often mistaken for either a local citizen or a prominent Vietnamese visitor. At one point, two old women asked Norasingh, who was wearing a silk shawl given to him by the local Buddhist lama, for a blessing. Norasingh put aside his cameras for a few minutes and obliged in fluent Laotian.
Photographer:
Seny Norasingh, USA

● *Left*

Bella Abovskaya, a student at
the Odessa School of Music.
Photographer:
Andy Levin, USA

● *Above*

At a children's sports school in
Volgograd, gymnastics students
eagerly swing onto the high bar.
Combining normal grammar
schooling with rigorous gymnastics training, this school gave
photographer David Turnley an
insider's view of the system that
produced Olga Korbut and so
many other international cham-
pions. Sports schools give Soviet
coaches a way to develop talented
youngsters all across the country.
Photographer:
David C. Turnley, USA

● *Above*

On a balmy spring day in Siberia, retired senior engineer Aleksandr Vorobyov, 63, lifts an improvised barbell in a Novosibirsk park.
Photographer:
Douglas Kirkland, Canada

● *Right*

Sculptor Ivan Misko molds Olympic champion wrestler Aleksandr Medved's bearish physique in his Minsk studio. Misko's sculptures, vigorous and straightforward images of such Soviet heroes as astronauts and athletes, fall within the conservative Socialist Realism style of art. This style was officially imposed by Stalin in 1932. Though members of the Union of Soviet Artists can once again dabble in various innovations and abstractions that would have been condemned as decadent bourgeois individualism during the Stalin era, most "official" art remains representational in form and didactic in content.
Photographer:
Yuri Ivanov, USSR

Sireniki, RSFSR **Vladimir Vyatkin, USSR**

Arshanovo, RSFSR **Ivo Hadjimishev, Bulgaria**

Karataikha, RSFSR **Boris Babanov, USS**

Tbilisi, Georgian SSR **Stephanie Maze, USA**

Samarkand, Uzbek SSR **Gerd Ludwig, West German**

Moscow, RSFSR

Rick Smolan, US/

● *Above*

Accordion 101: Students at the Tallin Music School practice while Tchaikovsky looks on. The accordion is not traditionally Russian, and only became popular after World War II when the Baltic republics were annexed by the Soviet Union.
Photographer:
Raphaël Gaillarde, France

● *Right*

Adolescent attitude knows no boundaries. Here, Dima Ivanov takes time out from a game of "American" billiards (Americans call it eight-ball) at a poolhall near the beach in Odessa.
Photographer:
Andy Levin, USA

The *banya,* or bathhouse, is a steamy, convivial place of communal rejuvenation that has been a constant of Russian daily life since the 11th century. The traditional *banya* was a small, one-room log hut, located next to peasant *izby* (cottages). The ultimate *banya,* however, is Moscow's famous Sandunov Baths, the elegant Beaux-Arts building pictured here.

Inside the Sandunov Baths, the main staircase greets tired, dirty Muscovites as it always has, with a riot of plaster cherubs and rococo murals. An elderly pensioner collects the modest price of admission from Soviet Army officers, workers and bureaucrats, who then make their way into the wood-panelled dressing room.

The basic business of the baths is and always has been conducted with the clothes off—rank and status are relegated to hooks, where a colonel's uniform sags next to dirty work clothes. The *mylnaya,* or washing room, presents as primal a scene as can be found anywhere: naked bodies of astonishingly varied age and condition all vigorously pursuing a common goal—scouring off the accumulated dirt of daily life.

The heart of the *banya* is the *parilnya*, the steam room, where mere washing gives way to an almost mystical act of self-purification. The only sounds are the hiss of steam from the huge open furnace full of heated stones, and the *slap, slap* of *veniki* (birch twig bundles) against wet skin. (Birching the body promotes circulation, and gives the air a pleasant, woody fragrance.) The most vigorous flagellation occurs on graduated wooden platforms. With each step up, the temperature seems to become more unbearable. The effect is very different from the dry heat of Finnish-style saunas. Here the moisture makes the air feel considerably hotter and more stifling, especially when bathers toss bucket after bucket of water onto the stones to a chorus of *"potepleye!"*—literally "a

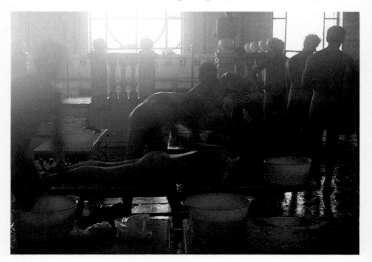

bit warmer" but actually meaning as hot as you can stand it.

Bathers seek relief from the inferno of the steam room with a plunge into the icy-cold water of the pool. Then comes the paradise of the dressing room, where much time is spent gossiping and arguing over plates of dried salted fish (to replace salt lost through perspiration) and the clandestine bottle of beer or vodka. There is no better place to experience daily life in the Soviet Union than among a group of men or women who, having purged the cares of the week from their bodies and souls, relax in the easy intimacy of the baths.

● *Previous page*

Patrons lather up in the *myl-naya*, or washing room, of the Sandunov Baths. There are showers along the wall, but the serious sudsing is done on these marble benches. Plastic buckets are available for washing, and most clients bring their own soap and shampoo.

The Ionic columns which ring the swimming pool are a striking reminder of the bath's pre-Revolutionary splendor. Con-trary to appearances, the water has been changed since the reign of Nicholas II—the green color comes from the fragrant birch leaves that stick to the skin after a session in the steam room.
Photographer:
Neal Slavin, USA

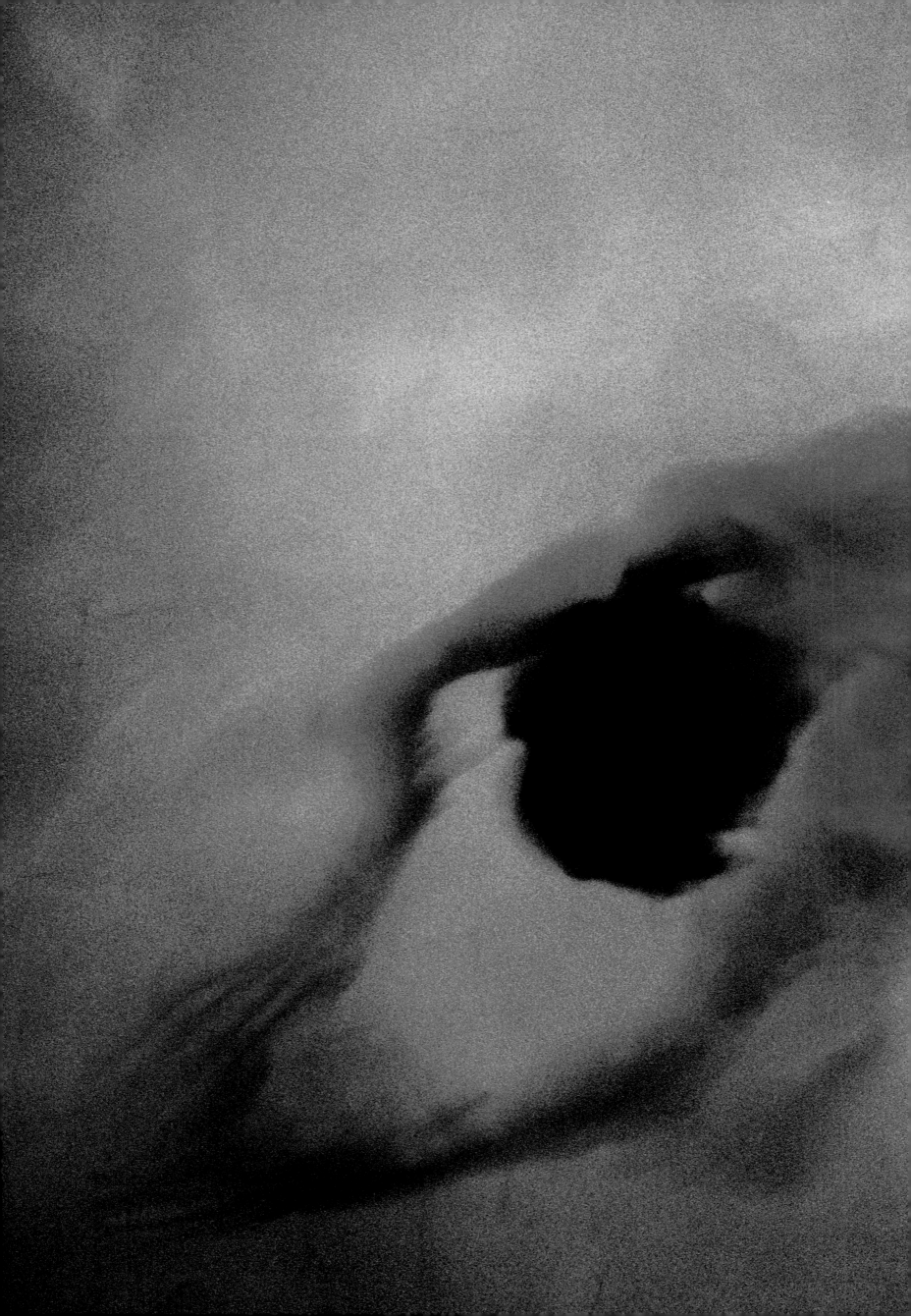

Bus riders in Khabarovsk endure *chas pik*—the Soviet rush hour. In a country with few private automobiles, public transportation plays a vital role. At five kopecks (about eight cents) a ride, it's a hard bargain to beat, except at *chas pik,* when demand for space often exceeds supply. Experts at fitting the maximum number of people into the smallest possible area, Soviets are accomplished pushers and shovers. The same frail *babushka* who totters unsteadily to the bus stop, demonstrates the strength and finesse of a seasoned linebacker when boarding the bus.
Photographer:
Dilip Mehta, Canada

● *Above*

Commuting Muscovites in the subway. Begun in the 1930s under the supervision of Stalin crony Lazar Kaganovich (and a young party official named Nikita Khrushchev), the ornate, ultra-efficent metro is one of the Soviet Union's proudest showpieces. The names of the stations read like a roll call of the nation's history: Marx Prospect, 1905 Street, October, Revolution Square, Lenin Library, et cetera.
Photographer:
Paul Chesley, USA

● *Following page*

A flight of fancy on the site of a half-built housing complex in the Troyeshchina district in suburban Kiev.
Photographer:
Oleg Homola, Czechoslovakia

Oleg Homola

● *Above*

Ambulance dispatchers wait for the next medical emergency in Baku. The dispatching system is similar to its American counterpart; however, unlike their colleagues in the US, Soviet doctors still make the occasional house call. May 15th was a slow night for accidents and injuries in this Caspian oil town of 1.7 million, and few ambulances were called out.

Photographer:
George Steinmetz, USA

● *Right*

Vladimir Zalensky cares for his bedridden wife. At 99, he is the oldest citizen of Krasnoyarsk, and has witnessed most of the major upheavals that have shaped the Soviet Union during the 20th century. He fought in World War I, the Revolution and the Civil War. Zalensky participates in local Communist Party activities, and posters with his portrait and words can be seen in many Krasnoyarsk streets. Old Bolsheviks like Zalensky, who have paid their historical dues, are amply rewarded with high pensions, low rent, free travel within the Soviet Union, free stays at health spas, treatment in the best hospitals and specially discounted food packages. According to photographer Solovyov, Zalensky's one complaint was that the local Party didn't give him enough volunteer work to do.

Photographer:
Feliks Solovyov, USSR

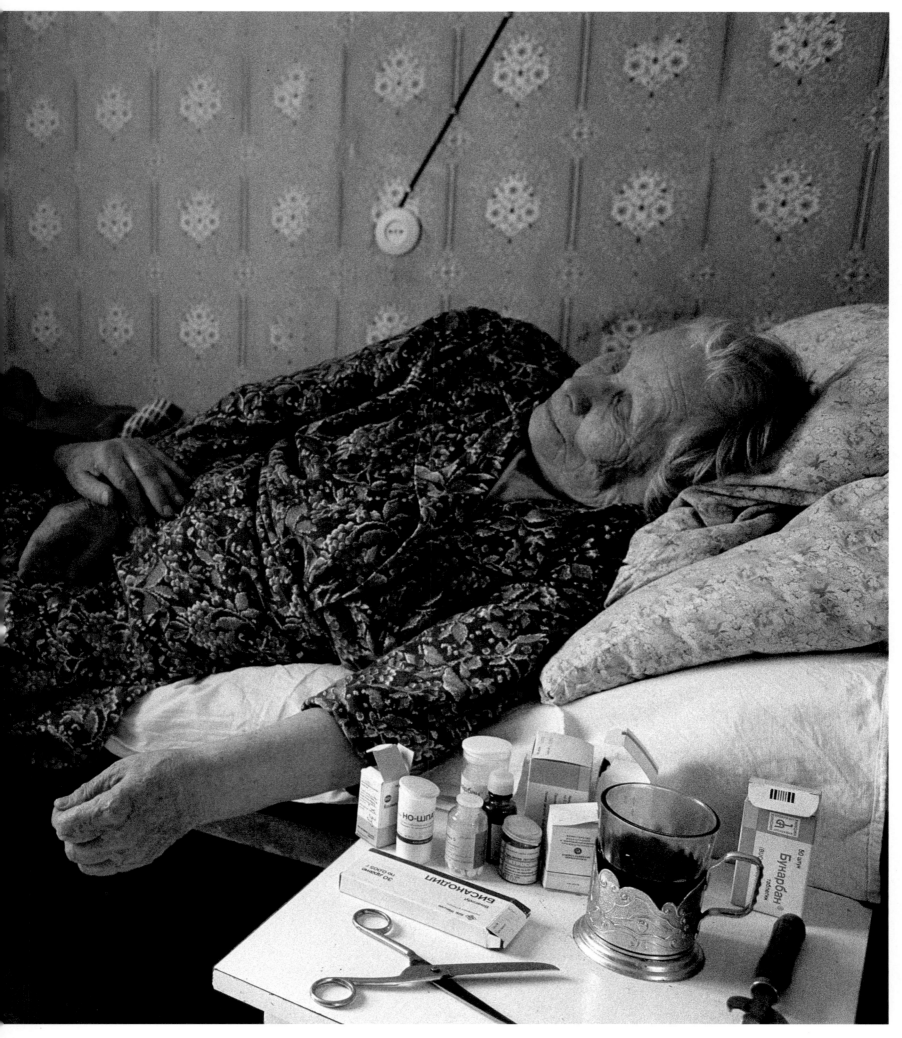

● *Above*

Army veteran Konstantin Tymchenko and his wife, Nina, pose for a double portrait-with-tulips in Volgograd.
Photographer:
David C. Turnley, USA

● *Right*

Nadya Tsagirishvili, 78, has been very lucky. She is one of an extraordinarily small group of women over 65 whose husbands are still alive. The Great Patriotic War (World War II) made millions of widows in her age group, as had the purges of the Stalin years. Here, Nadya and her husband, Severyan, celebrate a rare event—their 50th wedding anniversary—in their hometown of Tbilisi, Georgia.
Photographer:
Stephanie Maze, USA

● *Above, top*

A quiet afternoon at the Tbilisi home of Georgian film director Keti Dolidze.
Photographer:
Nikolai Gnisyuk, USSR

● *Above*

At home in their *balok* (mobile home) in Khatanga, Nganasan hunter Stepan Porotov and his wife, Vera, are like all doting parents.
Photographer:
Aleksandr Polyakov, USSR

● *Right*

May 15th was Nonna Pokrovskaya's birthday and she asked *Day in the Life* photographer Nicole Bengiveno to make a portrait of her and her son at the elegant Evropeiskaya Hotel in Leningrad.
Photographer:
Nicole Bengiveno, USA

● *Previous page*

Typy Bedotkin's responsibility in Soviet affairs is this herd of 600 Gorno-Altaiskiye goats grazing in the craggy foothills of the Altai Mountains in southern Siberia. A state farm oversees the raising, shearing and eventual slaughter of the special breed. Their downy undercoats are woven into winter parkas, and the goats' meat is used in local dishes.

Photographer:
James Balog, USA

● *Below*

Hunter-trapper Mikhail Degtyarev lives over 480 miles north of the Arctic Circle. He came to Dickson as a young boy in 1950 and now makes his living from the valuable pelts of sable and arctic fox. Northern Siberia is one of the last areas in the world where it is still possible to be a pioneer, and those who go voluntarily often find a great sense of freedom and opportunity far from the bureaucratic center. Though it was settled over 400 years ago, this small remote community along the northern sea route still has the feel of a frontier town.

Photographer:
Pavel Krivtsov, USSR

Time and tide wait for no man: Long shadows mark the end of a day at the beach at Sukhumi, a resort city on the eastern end of the Black Sea. The warmest, sunniest spot on the Black Sea, Sukhumi's parks and streets are lined with citrus, banana and palm trees. On May 15, 1987, the temperature reached 86° F.
Photographer:
Steve Krongard, USA

● *Above*

East is East: Eskimo children skip stones on the Bering Strait while waiting for their fathers and brothers to return home from the seal hunt. Only 80 miles separate the Eskimos of Sireniki from their kinsmen on St. Lawrence Island, Alaska.
Photographer:
Vladimir Vyatkin, USSR

● *Right*

And West is West: On a Baltic islet, Raina Laos and her schoolmates collect seagull eggs while their fathers are still at sea. The girls live in a small fishing community of 500 on the island of Kikhnu off the coast of Estonia.
Photographer:
Yuri Vendelin, USSR

● *Previous page*

Pedestrian underpasses honeycomb all major Soviet cities, providing shelter from fierce winters, refuge from tough laws against jaywalking and protection from drivers who rarely yield the right of way. Underground, pedestrians can find kiosks selling everything from lottery tickets to ice cream.
Photographer:
Nicole Bengiveno, USA

● *Left*

Naval cadets unwind at the Leningrad Military District Officers Club by following the example of the two gentlemen on the wall, realist writer Maksim Gorki and political strategist Vladimir Lenin. The lady is Lenin's wife and co-revolutionary, Nadezhda Krupskaya.
Photographer:
David Hume Kennerly, USA

● *Above*

In a quiet corner of the Armenian Orthodox Seminary in the ancient holy city of Echmiadzin, Grikhor Analyan, a third-year seminarian and piano student from Beirut, and Tatevos Asmaryan, his teacher, fine-tune a musical passage.
Photographer:
Oleg Makarov, USSR

● *Left*

A young woman makes an intercity call from a public telephone center in the town of Kazan. A long-distance call can be made from home in most large Soviet cities, and the rate, no matter how far the call, is relatively affordable. Directory information is harder to get, however. When the 1973 Moscow phone book went on sale, it had not been updated in 15 years, and only 50,000 copies were printed for what was then a city of nearly 7,000,000.

Photographer:
**Bernd-Horst Sefzik,
East Germany**

● *Above*

Georgians bearing gifts: These two young men carry lilacs in anticipation of a warm Friday evening in Tbilisi. Georgian men have the reputation of being the Don Juans of the Soviet Union —romantic and passionate or downright lewd, depending on which version of the stereotype you hear. When Moscow officials heard that *Day in the Life* was sending a female photographer to the Georgian capital, they were genuinely worried. But Stephanie Maze, a veteran of many Latin American assignments, handled this one with her customary aplomb.

Photographer:
Stephanie Maze, USA

● *Left*

The Rod-Stewart-coiffed lead guitarist of the amateur heavy-metal band, *Tir* (Rifle Range), takes center stage at an afternoon rock concert in Moscow's Gorki Park. The program includes rockabilly and ballads from the popular Bravo group and pop-rock from a slick, professional-sounding band called Lotus.

American photographer Bill Pierce decided he liked Bravo best, admiring the Russian tonalities in their music. He was less turned on by *Tir,* and said they were simply aping mainstream Western rock: "You can't imitate rich white people imitating young white people imitating old black people and take it across the ocean and have it be anything."

Photographer:
Bill Pierce, USA

t's more *fun* here now," says a oscow rock-and-roll journalist ho was once blacklisted for his ticles promoting underground ands.

Rock festivals, concerts and ubs have gone public—and ficial. Kids wear Led Zeppelin -shirts, leather jackets and ans. They travel to John Len- on birthday parties and sing Power to the People." Heavy- etal music screeches from apartment-block windows, and a big underground rock star, used to surveillance and official con- tempt, suddenly finds himself courted by state concert pro- moters, television producers and Melodiya Records, the most pro- minent record label in the USSR.

It all happened so fast—Gor- bachev's *glasnost* lifted the lid off the rock underground in 1986. Skeptics suggest that this liberalization is ultimately designed to coax alienated youth back into the arms of Soviet ideol- ogy. They say that the state is co- opting the Western-oriented rock scene to defuse the impact of underground bands and extend government control over the art form. Still, in the Soviet Union, the heart of rock and roll is beating louder than ever before.

Photographer:
Paul Chesley, USA

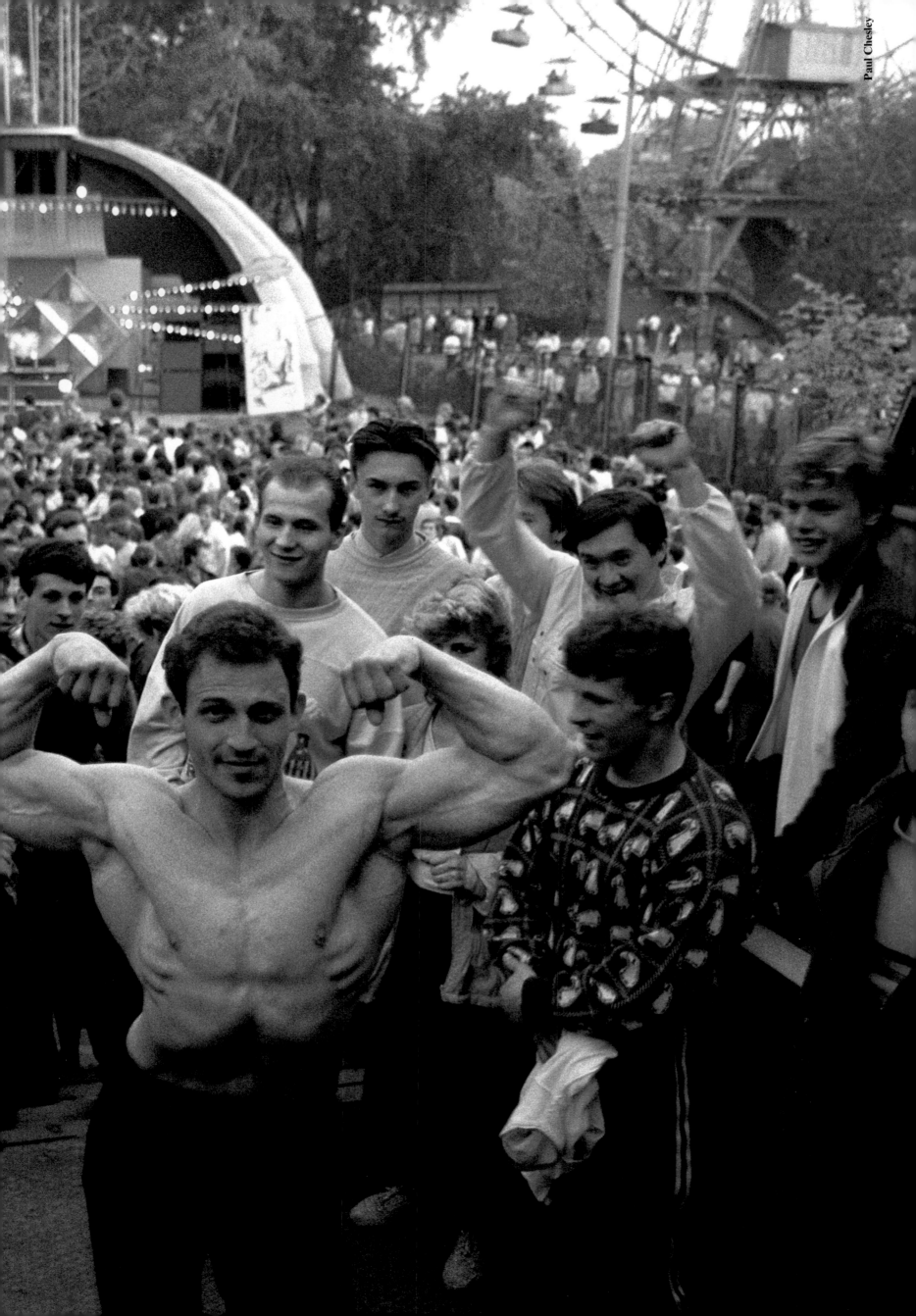

● *Previous page*

Double take in Gorki Park: In a strange coincidence, American photographer Paul Chesley snapped a picture of "Jail," the same young bodybuilder who had posed for another *Day in the Life* photographer earlier in the day in Lyubertsy (pages 136–37). Jail didn't seem to mind the attention in either case.
Photographer:
Paul Chesley, USA

● *Above, top*

Two Moscow punks in the apartment of their friend, an underground fashion designer. The young man told photographer Michael Benson that he had served a three-year prison sentence, and displayed his scars, claiming they were mementos of his jail term. While these punks would hardly ruffle a mohawk on London's King's Road, wearing a Nazi helmet is considered extremely offensive in a country that lost 20 million to the Nazis.
Photographer:
Michael Benson, USA

● *Above*

In Fili, a suburb of Moscow, an amateur band in heavy-metal drag rehearses in a small room provided for them by local authorities. Egg boxes on the walls act as acoustical tiles to deaden the sound. Photographer Nikolai Ignatiev noted that the session was interrupted by militiamen who politely asked the band not to smoke.
Photographer:
Nikolai Ignatiev, USSR

● *Above, top*

At their neighborhood ballroom in General Secretary Gorbachev's former home of Stavropol, Irina Semyokina 12, and Alex Balayev, 13, reach for maximum line and style as they swing into practice for stage two of the all-Soviet Union ballroom-dancing competition.
Photographer:
Wally McNamee, USA

● *Above*

Confidence man: Hands touch on the barre during dance class in Strezhevoi, central Siberia.
Photographer:
Sergei Edisherashvili, USSR

Backstage at the Bolshoi: On May 15th, the world's most prestigious ballet company was preparing for its 1987 tour of North America.
Photographer:
Vladimir Pcholkin, USSR

Kutbidin Atamkulov, 33, sings the epic tale of Manas, legendary hero of Central Asia's Kirghiz people. The mammoth 250,000-line song (By comparison, all of Homer is only 37,000 lines long.) was passed orally from master to student for centuries before it was finally written down in the early Soviet era. Atamkulov, who travels from one Kirghiz village to another singing *The Manas,* says that

for the first 15 minutes of the song, he must consciously remember the lines. "Then," he says, "I get into a trance, and it comes by itself. It's almost like watching a film. The story unrolls in my mind. If no one disturbs me, I can sing for 3 hours at a time from memory."
Photographer:
Frans Lanting, Netherlands

● *Above*

Sergei Shcherbina, a department
head at Gosplan, the State
Economic Planning Bureau,
relaxes at home in Moscow with
his cat and champion Afghan
hound, Vaska.
Photographer:
Torin Boyd, USA

● *Right*

Close friends: Writer Dina
Gurevich (right) chats with jazz
musician Manana Menabde during a get-together at Dina's
suburban Leningrad apartment.
Photographer:
Nicole Bengiveno, USA

● *Above*

In Tbilisi, Georgia, two-time
Olympic wrestling champion
and five-time world champion
Levan Tediashvili, 39, hoists
sons Vakhtang and Beso. After
the 1976 Montreal Olympics,
Tediashvili received the Order of
Lenin, the highest honor the
Soviet government can bestow
on one of its citizens.
Photographer:
Stephanie Maze, USA

● *Right*

Off the road: half a ton of
Moskvich parks atop a street
performer in Samarkand. Street
performances are an old tradition in Uzbekistan and other
parts of Central Asia. In the
past, performers would hire
themselves out to rich patrons or
perform for contributions from
passers-by. Now, the government
tolerates such displays, but pass-
ing the *doppi* (Uzbek hat) is
frowned upon. An evening stroll
in the local bazaar can still turn
up a variety of acts, from folk
plays, puppet theaters and
stand-up comedians, to dance,
acrobatics and feats of daring
like this one.
Photographer:
Gerd Ludwig, West Germany

● *Following page*

Late evening along Herzen Street in the old section of Moscow. Here, the street intersects the *Bulvarnoye Koltso,* a tree-lined circular boulevard that has retained its elegant, pre-Revolutionary character. The austere building at left is the Russian Orthodox Church of the Great Ascension, where Russia's most revered poet, Aleksandr Pushkin, was married in 1831. Further back stands the modern headquarters of the Soviet news agency TASS.

Photographer:
Roman Poderni, USSR

Roman Poderni

● *Above and above, top*

Showgirls in the dressing room of a Vilnius nightclub. The Baltic republics, including Lithuania, have strong cultural ties to Western Europe, and their capitals boast some of the hottest nightlife in the Soviet Union.
Photographer:
Dana Fineman, USA

● *Right*

Backstage at the Krasnoyarsk Theater of Opera and Ballet, Marina Kuznetsova, Olya Bylinkina and Ira Rastechayeva let down their hair after a performance.
Photographer:
Feliks Solovyov, USSR

● *Following page*

A well-worn segment of rail gleams under the lights of an approaching freight train near Birobidzhan, capital of the Jewish Autonomous Region in the Soviet Far East. A remote, swampy strip of land on the Chinese border set aside for Jewish settlement by Stalin in 1934, Birobidzhan did not prove to be the Promised Land, and Jewish settlers stayed away in droves. Today, they constitute less than ten percent of the population, but the region retains its official status, and signs at the train station greet Trans-Siberian passengers in both Cyrillic and Hebrew.

Photographer:
Graeme Outerbridge, Bermuda

● *Following pages 222–223*

At the Soviet-Iranian frontier, a searchlight scans the Caspian coastline, and a border guard keeps vigil with infrared night binoculars. The Soviets maintain a 15-mile restricted-access zone along their border with Iran, and every mile bristles with troops and high-tech hardware, supplemented in these parts by drug-sniffing dogs.

Photographer:
Vyacheslav Kiselyov, USSR

● *Following pages 224–225*

The domes of St. Basil's Cathedral provide the backdrop for a balmy Friday night on Red Square.

Photographer:
Larry C. Price, USA

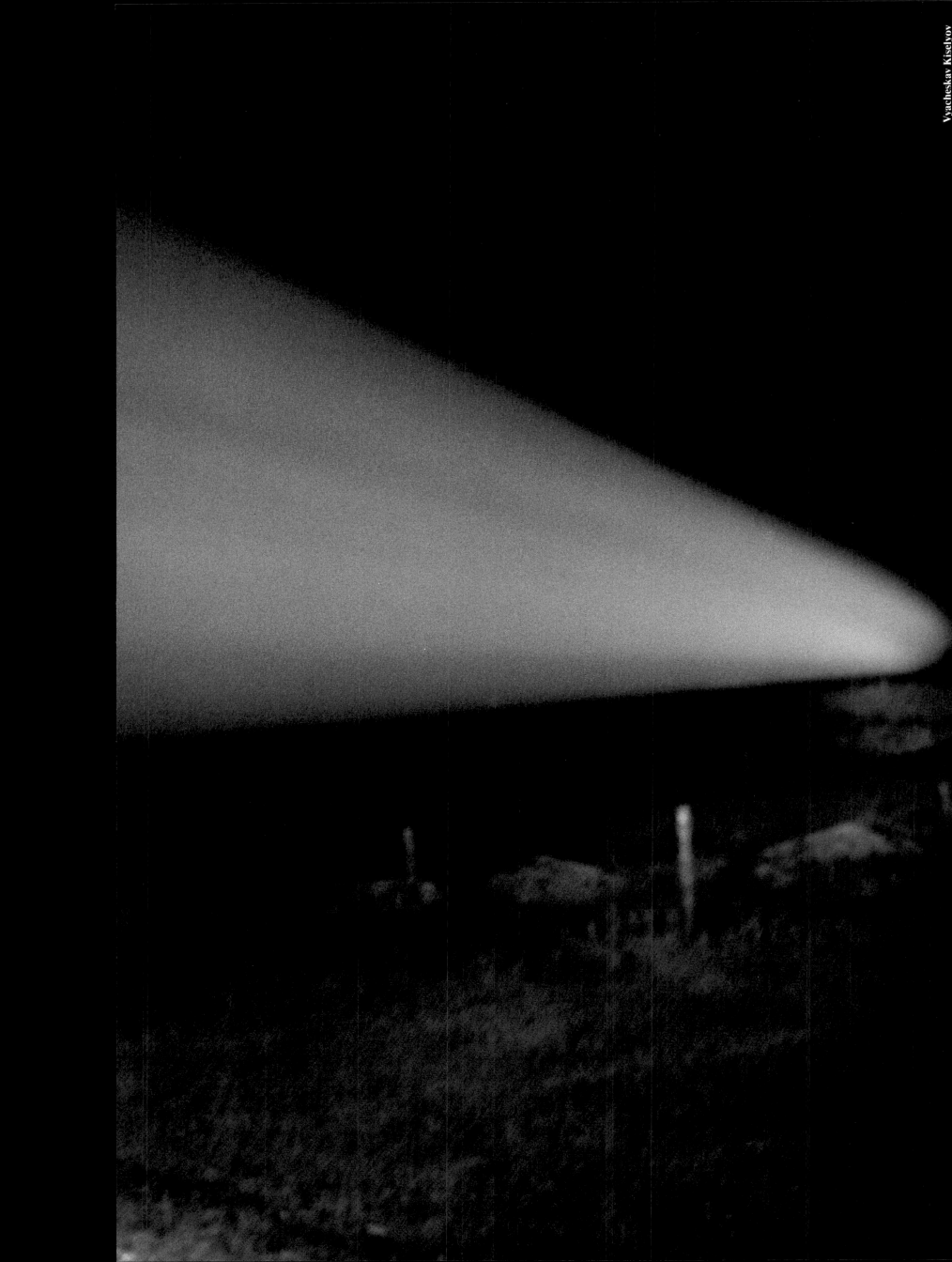

Photographers'
Assignment Locations

85°35'(N)1°05'(W)/107

● Dickson/54

● Murmansk/61

● Norilsk/37

● Vorkuta/73

● Arkhangelsk/28

● Tiltim/26

● Kazym/49

● Leningrad/29,50,65,89
● Narva/8

● Kirov/85

● Tallinn/6

● Kikhnu Island/7

● Novgorod/69

● Ustinov/52

● Surgut/80

● Riga/20

● Zagorsk/82
● Vladimir/24   ● Gorki/53   ● Cheboksary/25
● Star City/70   ● Kazan/74
★ Moscow/23,30,32,33,35,43,
         56,64,68,76,77   ● Ulyanovsk/46
● Peredelkino/87

● Narym/36

● Kaliningrad/81
● Vilnius/21

● Togliatti/84   ● Kurgan/88

● Minsk/5

● Voronezh/40   ● Saratov/55

● Omsk/48

● Kiev/96,99,100

● Akademgorodok/5

● Lvov/101   ● Poltava/93

● Dnepropetrovsk/95

● Volgograd/83

● Kishinev/22

● Elista/34

● Semipalatinsk/

● Sevastopol/98   ● Astrakhan/59
● Odessa/97 ● Yalta/94   ● Stavropol/57

● Baikonur/14

● Sochi/31
● Sukhumi/10

● Shevchenko/15

● Grozny/39
● Makhachkala/38

● Nukus/104   ● Chimkent/17   ● Alma Ata/13

● Tbilisi/9,11
● Batumi/12   ● Baku/4
● Yerevan/1,2

● Khiva/105   ● Frunze/18

● Tashkent/102

● Lenkoran/3

● Bukhara/106   ● Osh/19

● Samarkand/103

● Ashkhabad/92   ● Dushanbe/90

● Khorog/91

Letizia Battaglia

Two bundles of joy at an Arkhangelsk hospital.

Dirck Halstead

Math class in Lenin's hometown
of Ulyanovsk.

Graciela Iturbide

A Moldavian mother can't get the youngest of
her ten children to smile for the camera.

226

Peter Turnley

Tea time at an outdoor café in Bukhara.

John Vink

Herding sheep on a state farm in Kazakhstan.

Magsarym Tserenzhamts

Lvov's Goritsvet Dance Troupe.

Frank Fournier

Tashkent's Alaisky Market.

● Khatanga/67

● Sireniki/86

● Yakutsk/42

● Ust Ilimsk/60

● Krasnoyarsk/78

● Petropavlovsk Kamchatsky/66

● Abakan/45

● Tynda/72

Gorno Altaisk/27

● Komsomolsk na Amure/44

● Khabarovsk/58

● Yuzhno Sakhalinsk/41

● Birobidzhan/63

● Kyzyl/79

● Lake Baikal/71

● Ulan Ude/62

● Nakhodka/47

● Vladivostok/75

Armenian SSR
1 Jodi Cobb
2 Oleg Makarov

Azerbaijan SSR
3 Vyacheslav Kiselyov
4 George Steinmetz

Byelorussian SSR
5 Yuri Ivanov

Georgian SSR
6 Nikolai Gnisyuk
7 Steve Krongard
8 Stephanie Maze
9 Corneliu Mocanu

Estonian SSR
10 Raphaël Gaillarde
11 Yuri Vendelin
12 Marina Yurchenko

Kazakh SSR
13 Jean-Pierre Laffont
14 Aleksandr Mokletsov
15 Anatoli Morkovkin
16 Aleksandr Sentsov
17 John Vink

Kirghiz SSR
18 Dmitri Baltermants
19 Frans Lanting

Latvian SSR
20 Patrick Tehan

Lithuanian SSR
21 Dana Fineman

Moldavian SSR
22 Graciela Iturbide

Russian SFSR
23 Yuri Abramochkin
24 Eddie Adams
25 Vitali Arutyunov
26 Boris Babanov
27 James Balog
28 Letizia Battaglia
29 Nicola Bengiveno
30 Torin Boyd
31 Aaron Chang
32 Viktor Chernov
33 Paul Chesley
34 Anne Day
35 Dmitri Donskoi
36 Sergei Edisherashvili
37 Vladimir Fedorenko
38 Janusz Fogler
39 Gerrit Fokkema
40 Rudolf Frey
41 Igor Gavrilov
42 Diego Goldberg
43 D. Gorton
44 Fridrikh Grinberg
45 Ivo Hadjimishev
46 Dirck Halstead
47 Frank Johnston
48 Boris Kaufman
49 Yuri Kaver
50 David Hume Kennerly
51 Douglas Kirkland
52 Gennadi Koposov
53 Yuri Korolyov
54 Pavel Krivtsov
55 Vladimir Lagranzh

56 Sarah Leen
57 Wally McNamee
58 Dilip Mehta
59 Claus C. Meyer
60 Rogelio Mor
61 Jan Morek
62 Seny Norasingh
63 Graeme Outerbridge
64 Bill Pierce
65 Valeri Plotnikov
66 Sergei Podlesnov
67 Aleksandr Polyakov
68 Larry C. Price
69 Nikola Radosevic
70 Roger Ressmeyer
71 Galen Rowell
72 Viktor Rudko
73 Sergei Samokhin
74 Bernd-Horst Sefzik
75 Lev Sherstennikov
76 Neil Slavin
77 Rick Smolan
78 Feliks Solovyov
79 Yuri Somov
80 Vladimir Syomin
81 Jan Tikhonov
82 Tomasz Tomaszewski
83 David C. Turnley
84 Jerry Valente
85 Viktor Velikzhanin
86 Vladimir Vyatkin
87 Grace Kennan Warnecke
88 Lajos Weber
89 Mark Wexler

Tajik SSR
90 Jim Richardson
91 Vladimir Rodionov

Turkmen SSR
92 Sebastio Salgado

Ukrainian SSR
93 Jay Dickman
94 Arthur Grace
95 Sergei Guneyev
96 Oleg Homola
97 Andy Levin
98 Aleksandr Makarov
99 Mary Ellen Mark
100 Matthew Naythons
101 Magsarym Tserenzhamts

Uzbek SSR
102 Frank Fournier
103 Gerd Ludwig
104 Vladimir Perventsev
105 Andrew Stawicki
106 Peter Turnley

Arctic Ocean
107 Vladimir Chistyakov

A Day in the Life of the Soviet Union Revisited

Valeri Plotnikov

Frank Johnston

Come and keep your comrade warm: The Moscow staff pauses for a well-deserved breather (from left, standing): Lew Stowbunenko, Mark Rykoff, Patti Richards, Grace Kennan Warnecke, William McCabe, David Cohen, Devyani Kamdar, Boris Polkhovsky, Marina Yurchenko, D. Gorton, Eugene Zykov; (seated, rear) Torin Boyd, Sergei Nikitenko, Valeri Golubtsov; (kneeling) Nick Louis, Jean-Christophe Castelli.

Dirck Halstead

They arranged for me to photograph a welder and his family at home in their apartment. I looked at the guy's hands while he was talking, and it was obvious he was not a welder. The lifestyle didn't look like the way a welder would live. There was a big stereo, a big-screen TV and all the rest. I'm sure he was a Party member—the family was very well-to-do.

When we got back, I had a long frank talk with my guide. I told him I was annoyed at the time I had spent in situations that seemed set-up. He asked which things I thought had been faked for my benefit. I said the welder was obviously not a welder. He agreed. He said he had been very angry at the local guide for the whole episode. He said that this was exactly the sort of thing that destroyed Soviet credibility with the foreign press.

Nicole Bengiveno

I started photographing a woman working at the children's café in Leningrad, and when I was introduced to her she started to cry. I thought I had done something to offend her, but when I asked my interpreter, she said the woman was just overwhelmed at meeting an American. She said it brought up feelings from World War II when the Americans and Soviets were fighting on the same side. The whole thing caught me by surprise, and I started to cry, too. It was one of those things where we just hugged each other. I didn't get it on film but it's something I'll remember for a long long time.

The Soviet Union is probably the most talked-about yet least-visible place on earth: it is a country of more than one hundred nationalities, of immeasurable richness and depth, of cities deeply scarred by history and huge areas untouched by human habitation. But the familiar stock of images—food lines, Lenin posters, the Politburo waving a stiff benediction over a row of tanks on Red Square—is little more than a shelf full of dusty old icons and meaningless preconceptions. *Every* departing Moscow bureau chief comes out with his or her memoir about the "real" Russia, but no Western photographer has managed to make a decent photographic portrait of the country in years.

The Soviet Union is radiantly photogenic—the final proof is in these pictures—but it is also morbidly camera-shy. This is truly a country where a picture is worth a thousand words—words of warning, that is. Take this passage from the Intourist pamphlet *Rules for Photographing and Filming in Soviet Territory:*

It is prohibited to photograph, film or make drawings of all kinds of military hardware and military objects, seaports, large hydroengineering works, railway junctions, tunnels, railway and motorway bridges, industrial enterprises, scientific research institutes, design offices, laboratories, power stations, radio beacons, telephone and telegraph exchanges.

It is prohibited to take pictures from planes, to take long-range overland pictures and make drawings within the 25 km border zone. . .

A writer can rummage around for superlatives in the safety of his own mind. The photojournalist, on the other hand, has to reach into his camera bag, and by the time he has pulled out his Nikon F3, an irate *babushka* is yelling "*ne nado*" (literally "it's not necessary," really meaning "buzz off, buster") and the local militia have already been alerted.

This scenario—multiplied by 50 excitable Western photojournalists, several hundred suspicious militiamen and a thousand confiscated rolls of Kodachrome—haunted the *Day in the Life of the Soviet Union*

(DITLOSU) staff from day one. Would the Soviet Union really open its doors, or would the photographers be shown a series of facades, updated Potemkin villages?

Well, the doors did swing open, not without a squeak or two of protest from the occasional rusty hinge, but enough to let in a group of the world's finest photojournalists. They were given unprecedented access, and they brought back the most comprehensive visual record of life in the Soviet Union ever published in the West. *A Day in the Life of the Soviet Union* is the story of how an impossible dream in the heads of project co-directors Rick Smolan and David Cohen became the reality you hold in your hands. There's an historical dimension as well to this particular photo album. It captures an ordinary day, but it reflects an extraordinary period of change in the Soviet Union. Gorbachev's policy of *glasnost,* or openness, is the guiding spirit behind DITLOSU and it was this policy, still in its hesitant first stages, that made such a project even thinkable.

It all started with a closed door back in the early pre-*glasnost* days of 1984, when photojournalist Rick Smolan and editor David Cohen dropped by the Soviet Embassy in Washington, D.C. with an introduction from *National Geographic* editor Bill Garrett and an exceedingly strange book proposal. Smolan had some impressive achievements to his name. A few years earlier, he had had this crazy idea of sending 100 of the world's best-known photojournalists across Australia and having them all shoot pictures during a single day. The result, *A Day in the Life of Australia,* sold more than 200,000 copies worldwide. His partner, David Cohen, formerly the managing editor of the New York photo agency Contact, joined Smolan in putting together a sequel, *A Day in the Life of Hawaii* (December 2, 1983). Perhaps the Soviet Union did not seem a logical follow-up to a small Pacific paradise. At any rate, the people at the embassy listened politely, and said they would get back to the two youthful publishers. They didn't. Smolan and Cohen later found out the Soviets thought they were too young and didn't come across as businessmen.

But some people just won't take *nyet* for an answer. Like persistent salesmen, Smolan and Cohen came calling again in the fall of 1984 with the bestselling *A Day in the Life of*

228

...ces of spades: Deputy chairman of the
...ovosti Press Agency Georgi Fedyashin,
...ets some help from project directors
...ick Smolan and David Cohen at a tree-
...lanting ceremony in Moscow's Park of
...ulture.

Stephanie Maze

Rick Smolan

And it works even better with the lens cap off: A budding Soviet cameraman picks up a few tips from *Denver Post* photographer Jay Dickman. Sony supplied each Western photographer with an 8 mm Handicam.

Canada under their arms. Now that they had covered the second-largest country in the world, they were ready for the Soviet Union.

Instead, they ended up shooting *A Day in the Life of Japan*. Having negotiated the fearsome Japanese bureaucracy, crossed a language barrier and successfully penetrated a closed society, surely *now* they were ready for the Soviet Union. With four *Day in the Life* projects behind them, Smolan and Cohen even looked older. More usefully, *Time* magazine picture editor Arnold Drapkin, a veteran of several *Day in the Life* projects, put in a few good words on their behalf on one of his visits to Moscow.

But still there was no definite response. So in a fit of pique, Smolan and Cohen undertook one of the most ambitious projects in the history of photojournalism: on May 2, 1986, they orchestrated *A Day in the Life of America*.

About this time, Smolan and Cohen were joined in their dogged pursuit of a Soviet scoop by Ira Shapiro, publisher of the *American Showcase* series of photography and illustration graphics annuals. Shapiro's approach to the project was more idealistic than *Day in the Life*'s let's-see-how-we-can-top-this-one attitude. He imagined *A Day in the Life of the Soviet Union* as a bridge of understanding between the two superpowers. Shapiro had made two trips to the Soviet Union at his own expense to initiate the negotiations. And whenever Smolan and Cohen started to give up on the book, Shapiro was always there, urging them to try one more time.

In the fall of 1986, the *troika* took a trip to Moscow for serious negotiations with the official Soviet press agency, Novosti. After a day of meetings, two things became obvious: first, that Smolan and Cohen would never get remotely favorable terms to do *A Day in the Life of the Soviet Union,* and second, that they couldn't find a restaurant in their own hotel that would serve them—a bad omen for a project that would require some of the most staggering logistical planning this side of the first Five Year Plan. Still, Felix Rosenthal, a veteran of *Time* magazine's Moscow bureau, told them not to give up hope, and they didn't.

In fact, only a few weeks later everything started falling into place: the *glasnost* campaign in Moscow began to pick up steam; *A Day in the Life of America* shot to the top of *The New York Times* bestseller list where it remained in orbit longer than the Soviet Mir space station; and on Christmas Day 1986, unbeknownst to Smolan and Cohen, a group of US schoolchildren presented General Secretary Gorbachev with *A Day in the Life of America,* proving that there is a Santa Claus.

Suddenly, Smolan, Cohen and Shapiro were able to weave all the Soviet red tape into some semblance of a red carpet. The ratio would be 50 Western photographers and 50 from the Soviet bloc, chosen by Collins Publishers and approved by Novosti. There would be no editorial interference from Novosti in the final selection of images for the American edition, and complete freedom for the Soviets to produce their own version. And then the deal-maker: Novosti agreed that all the film shot on the day could be taken out of the Soviet Union *undeveloped*.

Novosti wanted the book out in the fall of 1987 to commemorate the 70th Anniversary of the Great October Revolution. Collins' sales staff, led by Carole Bidnick and Debbie Donnelly, heartily agreed. A good capitalist, Bidnick realized that Red October coincided with White Christmas, the height of the bookselling season.

The problem was that Smolan and Cohen, thinking that they would once again be stalled by the Soviet Union, were already committed to producing *A Day in the Life of Spain*. To pursue both projects would involve shooting, editing and laying out two books in a period of time that was absurdly short even for one—as publicity director Patti Richards was heard to mutter, "*Two* terrible concepts in one!" To beleaguered art director Tom Walker, the prospect of designing two multi-million-dollar extravaganzas at once conjured up nightmarish visions of chaos in the layouts, of flamenco dancers exiled to Siberia and the Soviet Army overrunning Seville. But Smolan and Cohen, masters at harnessing chaos, looked at it this way: why not? In fact, thanks to the organizational skills of project manager Cathy Quealy and the hard work of the Spain staff, the Madrid office proved to be an invaluable base of operations for the Soviet project as well.

William Collins, the British publishing house, rolled its eyes at yet another folly from its young American entrepreneurs, and like a good parent company, agreed to back a project that was essentially in the red (as it were) from the

Eric Lars Bakke

Ladies of Spain (plus one): The support staff in Madrid provided the Moscow office with invaluable help. They are (left to right, seated): Amy Janello, Fernando de Miguel Muñoz, Marie-Claire Rodriguez Dulin, Laura Lowenthal, Karen Bakke; (standing) Jennifer Erwitt, Cathy Quealy.

Rick Smolan

Arthur Grace

Contrary to my expectations, I wasn't hassled in the slightest. Quite the opposite; everybody was more than friendly. No one was posing for the camera or putting it on. I had more freedom shooting here than I would have in the United States. More people would have complained there than here. As far as I could tell, these people weren't briefed or told anything about who I was. How could they have faked an entire beach resort? I basically photographed average Russians on holiday at the beach. No one can convince me otherwise. It was very easy, and the people were extremely photogenic. It couldn't have been any easier.

Matthew Naythons

My guide, Valeri, was a very nice guy. Very professional, very pleasant, very charming, a Party member. It was his job to make me feel at home. But he was a presence. You'd have to be blind, apolitical and self-delusory to think this doesn't have an effect on you. They all have the reputation for working for the intelligence community, and you'd be foolish if you thought that wasn't true. If you believe that these guys are just good buddies, then their strategy is effective. The best part of that strategy is that they really try to charm you and make you like them so much that you don't want to offend them or get them in trouble. That's the psychology behind their warmth. These gentlemen are absolute professionals. I have tremendous respect for the public relations and intelligence side of this country. These guys are total pros. There are photographers out there totally in love with their guides and translators; they don't realize the grand game that's being played. I found it amusing.

Troika treat: Photographers Torin Boyd and D. Gorton help associate publisher Ira Shapiro hunt for photos in downtown Moscow.

start. By publishing standards, the *Day in the Life* books boast Spielbergian budgets—*A Day in the Life of the Soviet Union* cost a cool two and one-half million rubles (four million dollars). Smolan and Cohen have always relied on the kindness of major corporations for financing and services, but in the case of this project, sponsorship was a problem—after all, in the Soviet Union, the government itself is the only major corporation. American Express, a generous sponsor of past *Day in the Life* projects, said to leave home without them. Efforts to shake up the cola wars between Coke and Pepsi fizzled. And so *A Day in the Life of the Soviet Union* was launched with the backing of only four companies—Kodak, Nikon, Pan Am and Sony—instead of the usual ten.

Finding 50 of the world's top photographers to fill the bill was less of a problem; as news about the project spread along the photojournalistic grapevine, *they* called *Day in the Life* for a change. It was the assignment of a lifetime, one at which even the most jaded lensmen jumped, though they kept jumping from different locations, driving flight coordinator Karen Bakke quietly crazy.

The project was now ready to go, and on April 2, 1987, a small, nervous group of *Day in the Life* staffers finally hit Soviet soil. After weathering the passport control in Moscow's International Airport, the shaky collective watched as over 100 boxes came out onto the luggage claim. This was the Moscow office in its entirety—seven people gathered together under the leadership of project co-director David Cohen, plus Apple computers, copying machines, stationery, pens, and American souvenirs. The Soviets customs officers were not amused.

Just when it seemed like the best option for the DITLOSU group was to disavow any knowlege of their mission and hop the next plane back to Frankfurt, a delegation from the Novosti Press Agency came out to greet them, all dazzling smiles and hearty handshakes. In less time than it takes to find a cab at Kennedy, they had bypassed customs and were on their way to a dinner featuring an endless supply of caviar and vodka, and repeated toasts to the radiant future of the project.

At any rate, it was the beginning of an eight-week-long crash course in the Soviet way of getting things done. The first rule of thumb was, *problemy nyet:* don't worry, anything could be fixed. The second rule was that what couldn't (or wouldn't) be fixed could be washed away with liberal toasts to the success of the project. The third rule was, everything is not what it seems. In fact, almost nothing was.

But neither the atmosphere of goodwill nor the constantly shifting realities of the project could conceal the tremendous hard work of the Soviet men and women who risked more than can readily be appreciated to turn this bizarre *glasnost* test case into a reality. The labors of dozens of people and several agencies rested squarely on the broad Russian shoulders of the three Novosti officials assigned to work full time on the project. Eugene Zykov (whose official title at Novosti was senior scientific editor) brought an inexhaustible supply of charm and diplomatic skill to every aspect of his work—not least of all his interpreting (Cohen: "This is *absolutely* unacceptable." Zykov

If these don't come out, you'll be seeing a lot more of me: Boris Babanov on assignment in Siberia.

in Russian: "David is saying sorry, but things are perhaps a little unsatisfactory right now...."). Boris Polkhovsky, a Soviet bulldog of a man, lined up literally hundreds of permissions with the aid of only one assistant and that none-too-reliable instrument, the Soviet phone. Sergei Nikitenko maintained an air of Buddha-like calm through even the worst of times, such as two days before the photographers' arrival on May 10th, when it was discovered that all 50 visas weren't valid for entry until May *11th*. Nikitenko fixed that, and got the staff vote as best-connected Russian, though no one knew how or why he was so well connected, or even cared after a while.

If the *Day in the Life* crew could teach the Soviets anything in return, it was how *not* to take things too seriously. The crew were hopelessly, gleefully out of place in the sleek, sober Mezhdunarodnaya Hotel, Moscow's answer to the Atlanta Hyatt—especially editorial coordinator Torin Boyd, whose day-glo surfer shirts vied with St. Basil's for the title of the brightest object in Moscow.

The assignment research started with a long list of cities and subjects proposed by Novosti, ranging from the sublime ("Chernobyl a year later") to the ridiculous ("a young rancher bottle-feeds a newly born mink at the Push-kino Fur-Production Farm"). The assignment team of D. Gorton, Bill McCabe, Mark Rykoff and Grace Warnecke countered with their own long list of suggestions, many of which must have seemed even more bizarre to the Russians ("Secretary General Gorbachev relaxing at home with his family" and "the most notorious prison in the USSR"). Scouting 8,646,400 square miles in five weeks was pretty much out of the question, so the editors drew on their journalistic experience (Gorton was an editor of *A Day in the Life of America*), their expertise in Soviet affairs (Rykoff and McCabe were Columbia-trained Soviet experts) and some inspired guesswork (Warnecke grew up in the American Embassy in Moscow). Gaining access to closed areas and subjects was like an elaborate game of five-card stud—"I'll see your Jewish Autonomous Region and raise you a nuclear power plant..." —with one catch: the Soviets had most of the cards and all the chips. Gracious hosts that they were, they let us win a few rounds anyway.

Need 120,000 pictures edited in one weekend? Call the DITLOSU photo-editing team (left to right, standing): Felix Rosenthal, Don Abood, Anatoli Bogomolov, Stephanie Maze, Yuri Zodiev, Alfonso Gutiérrez Escera, Dieter Steiner, Kent Kobersteen, Mark Grosset, Tom Walker; (seated) Aleksei Pushkov, Arnold Drapkin, Eliane Laffont, Jennifer Erwitt. Ruth Eichhorn was still editing when this photo was taken.

As May 15th, the day of the shoot, approached, *Odin den iz zhizni Sovetskovo Soyuza* (as the project is known in Russian) started attracting all sorts of attention around town. The Soviets proved as adept as their American counterparts at whipping up a media circus. *Sovetskaya kultura, Izvestiya* and *Komsomolskaya pravda* don't exactly play in Peoria, but the circulation figures (over 40 million for *Komsomolskaya pravda* alone) were enough to impress even Patti Richards, a survivor of three *Day in the Life* media blitzes. After a few minutes of talk about peace and world understanding, Cohen would lean back and say to each interviewer: "You know, first and foremost, I'm a businessman. I want this book to sell three hundred thousand copies. . . ." The Soviets, who traditionally respect businessmen and big numbers, were clearly impressed.

Crews from ABC News' "20/20" and NBC's "Today Show" were also on hand for the arrival of Smolan and the Western photographers which—thanks to Nikitenko—proceeded without a hitch. Next to their Western counterparts, the Eastern-bloc photographers—most from Moscow and some from as far away as Ulan Bator, Mongolia and Havana, Cuba—presented a disconcerting contrast. Here they were, professional lensmen at the top of their fields, and yet they lacked the one piece of equipment always associated with photojournalists—outsized egos.

The mood at the opening ceremony was one of barely suppressed excitement, mixed with a feeling of nervousness. For many of the Soviet photographers, it would mean their first exposure to Western audiences. And for the Western photographers, it was a chance to test the limits of the acceptable. But as Cohen put it to the assembled crowd at Moscow's Intourist Hotel: "If you think you're scared, just imagine how your hosts must feel!"

In the end, the worst-case scenario (a long-distance call from the Ulan Ude police station) was averted. A multilingual group of 65 Novosti editors and reporters (some of whom looked like they might answer to the Russian word for "lieutenant") kindly took a couple of days off from their busy careers to keep the photographers—and Novosti—out of trouble on location. Despite its resemblance to a cereal box prize, the official *Day in the Life of the Soviet Union* I.D. badge usually transformed the most stubborn "*nyet!*" to an effusive "It's for the photo album? Well, why didn't you say so!" Many of the photographers took along 8 mm video cameras provided by Sony, bringing back unique footage of places no Western camera crews had ever visited.

By the time the photographers had flown to their locations, news of the project had spread to every corner of the Soviet Union. As a result, many of the photographers found themselves treated like celebrities. Elaborate feasts of local delicacies like goat's head and fermented mare's milk awaited them. Very few were detained, except for just one more drink, and all of the Western photographers came back on time. Some of the more far-flung Soviets took a bit longer (at the time of writing, one of them is still on an icebreaker near the North Pole). They were train- and jet-lagged, gaunt from all the running around, or ten pounds overweight from too much conviviality. Their reactions varied from ecstatic to frustrated—often both at the same time—but indifference was never part of it, and it shows in almost every one of the 127,000 frames that came back from May 15th.

After several days of round-the-clock vigilance by logistics coordinator Lew Stowbunenko, the boxes of film were whisked through Sheremetevo. But only when the boxes were comfortably strapped into the wide seats of Pan Am's first-class flight to Frankfurt, did the Western photographers let out a single whoop of relief—their last collective act before resuming their erratic, solitary wanderings (until the next invitation from Smolan and Cohen).

A few days later in Madrid, a team of top picture editors, including three Soviets, and assisted by film coordinator Jennifer Erwitt, distilled the essence of a 240-page book out of a bewildering number of images. So *this* was the Soviet Union—not the gray monolith of the news magazines, but an infinitely varied and colorful nation.

Among these frames are the "forbidden" pictures: former White House photographer David Hume Kennerly shot dozens of soldiers; Frank Johnston of *The Washington Post* captured a seaport; Graeme Outerbridge was one of many photographers with pictures of railway junctions; Jerry Valente shot a mighty industrial enterprise; Hollywood photographer Douglas Kirkland roamed at will in scientific research institutes, design offices and laboratories; Austrian Rudolf Frey went to a nuclear power station; and David Turnley of *The Detroit Free Press* boarded a helicopter and took that ultimate *ne nado,* an aerial shot.

For better or worse, the idea of "unprecedented access" will be a great part of the mystique of *A Day in the Life of the Soviet Union*—and there are some remarkable images from places where no Westerners have ever been permitted to photograph. But what does this book reveal in the end? If it is successful, it shows that a train station is a train station—even when it can only be photographed with special permission from the proper authorities. You see people rushing with heavy suitcases, a young mother dozing on a bench while waiting for the Trans-Siberian, Soviet Army recruits kissing their loved ones goodbye . . . all the ordinary scenes which, when caught through the lens of a master photographer, reveal the pulse of common humanity in this country—or any country.

—Jean-Christophe Castelli

Steve Krongard

To me, the name of this book should be "Detained but not Arrested in the Soviet Union." Every time I asked my Novosti guide to ask for permission for me to take pictures, my subject would refuse. Even when I would carefully explain why I wanted to take his or her photograph, the person would often look at me and walk away. I began to think the whole country was rude, and I couldn't wait to get out of there. This was brutally difficult work. Every time things started going well, a cop would show up and start hassling me. This was not the right frame of mind to shoot in.

As the day wore on, I finally started to get some nice shots and I started enjoying the country more. At dinner that evening, my guides and I felt we'd been through an incredible experience together and we toasted each other well into the night. I experienced a feeling of well-being and euphoria that I have experienced rarely in my life.

David C. Turnley

During the course of the day my guides and I learned a lot from each other. We had some frank discussions and we hugged when we parted. At one point during the day, we were driving by a queue of people waiting to buy liquor in a store and I told the guides to stop the car. One of the guides said no. I insisted. He said the people in line would give me a hard time. I told him that I had been in South Africa for the past two years and I was used to people giving me a hard time. He was still reluctant. I got angry and insisted they stop the car. They did; I got the pictures.

When I got back in the car, the guide from Moscow said that while I was gone, the two guides had a discussion. They both had different points of view. The Moscow guide sided with me and thought the queue was an interesting situation for a photographer. The guy from Volgograd said that he was patriotic, and that the queue wouldn't be a nice thing for me to show. He admitted that it was difficult adjusting to more openness.

Sofia's choice: Bulgarian photographer Ivo Hadjimishev fraternizes with the natives in Abakan, central Siberia.

Undercover: Steve Krongard makes a trunk call while on assignment in the resort town of Sukhumi.

It's a long way from Havana: Cuban photographer Rogelio Moré enjoys an idol moment on assignment in Ust Ilimsk, Siberia.

Photographers' Biographies

Yuri Abramochkin

Soviet Union

Yuri Abramochkin
Soviet/Moscow
Abramochkin has worked as a photojournalist for over 25 years and has been a member of Novosti Press Agency since 1961. He has participated in numerous international exhibitions and has shown his work in India, Syria and across Eastern Europe. His assignments have included numerous US-USSR summit conferences, as well as *A Day in the Life of America.* In 1986, Planet Publishers of Moscow published his monograph, *The Photography of Yuri Abràmochkin.*

Eddie Adams

Saigon   1969

Eddie Adams
American/New York, New York
Winner of the Pulitzer Prize and the Silver Grand Prix Award of the Advertising Association of Japan, Adams is one of the most decorated and published photographers in the United States with over 500 awards to his credit. He has photographed leaders in all fields, from heads of state to the superstars of film, sport and high fashion.

Vitali Arutyunov
Soviet/Moscow
A graduate of the school of journalism at Moscow State University, Arutyunov has been a correspondent for Novosti Press Agency since 1974. He was the recipient of a Gold Medal from World Press Photo in 1987 and has participated in Interpressphoto and other competitions and exhibitions.

Boris Babanov
Soviet/Moscow
Boris Babanov graduated from the journalism faculty of Moscow State University in 1973 and has since worked as a correspondent for Novosti Press Agency, as well as on the magazines *Sovetskoe foto (Soviet Photo)* and *Sovetsky sport (Soviet Sport).* He has often photographed in Siberia and the Soviet Far East, and in 1986 he completed a prizewinning series on Africa. He is the recipient of a Gold Medal from World Press Photo, a Bronze Medal from the Great Wall of China competition and other awards.

James Balog
American/Boulder, Colorado
Balog won the 1987 World Press Photo competition for nature and landscape photography, as well as several awards in the 1987 National Press Photographers Association contest. He is a frequent contributor to *National Geographic, Smithsonian* and *Time-Life* publications. The International Center of Photography in New York published Balog's first book, *Wildlife Requiem*, in 1986. His work has been exhibited widely in American art galleries and museums.

Dmitri Baltermants

Soviet Union   1941

Dmitri Baltermants
Soviet/Moscow
One of the most eminent photographers in the Soviet Union, Baltermants has worked in the profession since 1936 and gained wide recognition for his World War II combat pictures. Baltermants's work has been exhibited worldwide, incuding shows in Moscow, London, New York, Paris, Belgrade and Budapest. He has received numerous awards for his photography, and currently serves on the editorial board of *Ogonyok,* the Soviet Union's most popular illustrated weekly magazine.

Letizia Battaglia

Sicily   1983

Letizia Battaglia
Italian/Palermo
Based in Sicily, Battaglia is the publisher of *Fotografia,* a photographic magazine for women and a monthly magazine of photography, politics and culture. She also heads La Luna, a publishing house of literature, sociology and anthropology, and she is the artistic director of a gallery and school of photography in Palermo, Il Laboratorio D'If. Battaglia was previously a staff photographer for *L'Ora.* In 1985, she won the prestigious Eugene Smith Grant to continue a photographic project documenting the Mafia in Sicily.

Nicole Bengiveno
American/New York, New York
Bengiveno is a staff photographer at the *New York Daily News.* She previously worked with the *San Francisco Examiner* and was named Bay Area Photographer of the Year in 1979. In 1984, she won first place in the Associated Press sports photo contest. In 1985, she was a finalist for the W. Eugene Smith Award for her documentary work on the AIDS epidemic.

Torin Boyd *American/Tokyo*
Boyd began his career as a surfing photographer and then became a photojournalist for *Florida Today, The Orlando Sentinel* and UPI. Now based in Tokyo, he regularly publishes his work in *Winds, Shukan Asahi,* and *Friday,* and is affiliated with Gamma Press Images. Boyd's pictures have also appeared in *Newsweek, Time* and *L'Express,* and he has served on the editorial staffs of the past three *Day in the Life* projects.

Aaron Chang
American/San Diego, California
Chang is currently senior staff photographer for *Surfing* magazine. In 1982, he received the American Society of Magazine Photographers Award for Excellence and was named one of the top five sports photographers in the United States by *American Photographer* magazine. His work has appeared in *Newsweek, Stern, American Photographer, People* and *Gentlemen's Quarterly.*

Viktor Chernov
Soviet/Moscow
Viktor Chernov was born into a family of photographers, but only became a professional photojournalist in his middle age after working as a mechanic, a metalworker and a laboratory assistant. A member of the Novosti Press Agency, Chernov specializes in reporting and character sketches. He has received a Gold Medal and a Golden Eye Award, both from World Press Photo.

Paul Chesley

Alaska   1980

Paul Chesley
American/Aspen, Colorado
Chesley is a freelance photographer who has worked with the National Geographic Society since 1975 and travels regularly to Europe and Asia. Solo exhibitions of his work have appeared in museums in London, Tokyo and New York. His work has also appeared in *Fortune, Time, Esquire, GEO* and *Stern.*

Vladimir Chistyakov
Soviet/Moscow
Since 1984, Chistyakov has taken his cameras to the North Pole, through the Qara Qum Desert, into volcanic craters and the crippled Chernobyl nuclear power plant, and on a dogsled expedition over 6,000 miles across the Arctic. He has been a correspondent with the Novosti Press Agency since 1972, and has received awards from World Press Photo, Interpressphoto, the Union of Journalists of the USSR, and other competitions. Chistyakov's photographs of the Arctic can be seen in the book, *Man and the North.*

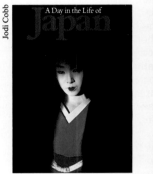
Jodi Cobb

A Day in the Life of Japan   1985

Jodi Cobb
American/Washington, D.C.
With a master's degree from the University of Missouri, Cobb has been a staff photographer for *National Geographic* since 1977. She has photographed major articles on China, Jerusalem, Jordan and London. In 1985, she was named the first woman White House Photographer of the Year. She was the subject of the Public Broadcasting Services television documentary, "On Assignment."

Anne Day
American/New York, New York
Anne Day is a freelance photographer who previously worked on *A Day in the Life of Japan* and *A Day in the Life of America.* Her work has been published in *Time, Newsweek, Fortune, The New York Times* and *Le Monde,* as well as in several books on architecture. In recent years, she has documented life in Haiti, Nicaragua and South Africa.

Jay Dickman
American/Denver, Colorado
Dickman was a newspaper photographer in the Dallas, Texas area for 16 years before moving to Colorado. His work has appeared in *National Geographic, Life, Time, Newsweek, Bunte, Stern, GEO* and other publications. He won a Pulitzer Prize in 1983, first place in the World Press Photo competition, the Sigma Delta Chi Award and many state and regional awards. He has served as a judge for a variety of photography contests and is a member of several prestigious regional and national photography associations.

Moscow   1980

Dmitri Donskoi
Soviet/Moscow
One of the Soviet Union's best-known sports photographers, Donskoi has worked at the Novosti Press Agency since 1962. He is the recipient of 146 awards from international photo competitions and holds the title International Master of Press-photography from the International Organization of Journalists. Donskoi also teaches a special seminar in sports photography at the prestigious journalism faculty of Moscow State University.

Sergei Edisherashvili
Soviet/Tbilisi, Georgian SSR
A native of Georgia, Edisherashvili was born in Tbilisi in 1951. He has worked in the press for 20 years and is the recipient of awards from the Interpressphoto competition, the international exhibition, "For the Art of Socialist Photography," and other Soviet and international events. Edisherashvili has shown his work in East Germany and Yugoslavia.

Vladimir Fedorenko
Soviet/Moscow
Fedorenko was born in 1949 in Moscow. Since his graduation in 1975 from the journalism faculty of Moscow State University, he has worked as a correspondent for Novosti Press Agency. He has exhibited his work in Poland and Madagascar and was awarded first place in the Great Wall of China photo contest in Beijing in 1986.

Terry Ferrante
American/New York, New York
Ferrante specializes in studio still-life photography for corporate clients such as *Newsweek*, Germaine Monteil, Black and Decker, Seiko watches, AT&T and Avon.

Dana Fineman
American/New York, New York
Fineman studied at the Art Center College of Design in Pasadena and worked for several years assisting celebrity photographer Douglas Kirkland. Her work appears in such publications as *New York, People, US, Stern, Time* and *Newsweek*. She is a member of the Sygma photo agency. On May 4, 1986, two days after the shooting of *A Day in the Life of America*, she married photographer Gerd Ludwig. Over 200 of the world's best photojournalists were on hand to cover the event.

Janusz Fogler
Polish/Warsaw
A graduate of the geography faculty of Warsaw University, Janusz Fogler is the head of publishing and journalism at MAW (the Youth Publishing Agency). His photographs have been published in France and Japan, and he has worked in the Middle East, France and Scandinavia. He has published a series of photography books on the USSR.

Gerrit Fokkema
Australian/Sydney
Fokkema is a freelance photographer who concentrates on both corporate and editorial assignments. He worked for 11 years on staff for several Australian newspapers including *The Sydney Morning Herald*. His work is included in the collections of the Australian National Gallery, the New South Wales Art Gallery and the National Library.

Columbia   1986

Frank Fournier
French/New York, New York
Fournier's work has appeared in a broad array of magazines and journals including *Time, Newsweek, Paris-Match, Stern, Life* and *The Sunday Times* (London). He won the premier award in the 1986 World Press Photo competition and is a member of New York's Contact Press Images.

Rudolf Frey
Austrian/Rome
After working as a television producer and freelance photographer, Frey joined *Time* magazine in 1978. Based in Rome, he covers the Mediterranean, the Soviet Union and the Vatican. He is the recipient of the Overseas Press Club's Robert Capa Award for his coverage of the Pope's visit to Poland in 1981.

Raphaël Gaillarde
French/Paris
Gaillarde is one of the leading news photographers of the Gamma agency. His in-depth coverage of world news events has appeared in many European magazines including *GEO*.

Igor Gavrilov
Soviet/Moscow
A 1975 graduate of the journalism faculty of Moscow State University, Gavrilov is a correspondent for *Ogonyok* magazine. He has participated in various Soviet photo exhibitions including "The 100th Anniversary of V.I. Lenin," "The 60th Anniversary of Great October" and "60 Years of Soviet Rule." He has also participated in the Interpressphoto, Europa and World Press Photo competitions.

Nikolai Gnisyuk

Moscow   1981

Nikolai Gnisyuk
Soviet/Moscow
Gnisyuk worked as a cameraman at the Riga Film Studio (Latvia) and is a member both of the Union of Journalists and the Union of Cinematographers. Since 1968, he has shot more than 250 covers and 2,500 photographs for the film magazine *Sovetsky ekran (Soviet Screen)*. Gnisyuk has exhibited his work throughout Eastern Europe, and is included in both the *Encyclopedia of Contemporary Photography* and the Swiss encyclopedia, *Kamera Obscura*.

Diego Goldberg
Argentine/Buenos Aires
After beginning his photographic career in Latin America as a correspondent for *Camera Press*, Goldberg moved to Paris in 1977 as a Sygma staff photographer. In 1980, he moved to New York and worked as one of Sygma's leading photographers for five years before returning to Argentina. His work has been featured in major magazines throughout the world, and in 1984, he won a World Press Photo Foundation prize for feature photography.

A Day in the Life of America   1986

D. Gorton
American/Cincinnati, Ohio
Gorton is a freelance photographer based in Cincinnati. He was the chief photographer of *The Philadelphia Inquirer*, and worked on the staff of *The New York Times* in New York and Washington, D.C., where he covered the White House and Capitol Hill. He was an assignment editor and photographer on *A Day in the Life of America* as well as *A Day in the Life of the Soviet Union*. His work has been published in *Stern, National Geographic, Smithsonian* and *People*.

Arthur Grace
American/Washington D.C.
Grace is a Washington-based staff photographer for *Newsweek* magazine. His work includes *Newsweek* cover stories on Governor Mario Cuomo of New York and comedian Robin Williams, as well as a one-man exhibition of his black-and-white photography entitled, "Art Attack." His photographs have been published in leading magazines worldwide during his 15-year association with the Sygma photo agency.

Fridrikh Grinberg
Soviet/Moscow
Grinberg graduated from the journalism faculty of Moscow State University and has worked at Novosti Press Agency since 1965. He has taken part in various Soviet and international competitions and has received prizes at exhibitions in the USSR, Canada, Spain and East Germany.

Sergei Guneyev
Soviet/Moscow
Guneyev graduated from the Moscow Institute of Aviation in 1973. Since 1977, he has worked at the Novosti Press Agency as a correspondent. He has been honored for his sports photography by World Press Photo, Adidas and Kodak.

Ivo Hadjimishev
Bulgarian/Sofia
Hadjimishev is the photography editor of the newspaper *Otechestvo (Fatherland)* and has worked in Europe, the USSR, the United States and Africa. Photographing people is his specialty, and he has exhibited his work in Bulgaria, Austria, the USSR, Holland and the UK.

Dirck Halstead
American/Washington, D.C.
Halstead's photographic career began when he was only 17 years old, with his coverage of the Guatemalan Revolution in 1954 for *Life*. In the past 30 years, he has covered the major news events of the world for UPI and *Time* magazine, including the Kennedy White House, civil rights struggles in the South, the Vietnam War and Watergate. He has been honored by the Overseas Press Club, the Pictures of the Year competition, the White House News Photographers Association and other competitions.

Oleg Homola
Czech/Prague
Homola is a photographer with the Czech magazine *Svet v obrazekh (The World in Pictures)*, where he specializes in color reporting. He was honored by the Mongolian government for his photo album of that country and has also received awards from World Press Photo, Interpressphoto and Humorphoto competitions. His photographs have been published in his native Czechoslovakia and abroad, and he was featured in the *1983 Photography Year Book* published in Great Britain.

Graciela Iturbide

A Day in the Life of America   1986

Graciela Iturbide
Mexican/Mexico City
Iturbide uses her camera to capture the poetry in life. She has published two books in Mexico and has exhibited her work in Paris, Zurich and the US.

Yuri Ivanov
Soviet/Minsk, Byelorussian SSR
Ivanov worked in a factory and served in the Soviet Army before joining the newspapers *Znamya yunosti (The Banner of Youth)* and *Sovetskaya Byelorossiya (Soviet Byelorussia)*. He has worked as a correspondent for Novosti Press Agency since 1965, and is the author of a series of photo books on Byelorussian cities.

Frank Johnston
American/Washington, D.C.
Johnston began his career with United Press International covering the Vietnam War, the civil rights movement and the Kennedy assassination. He joined *The Washington Post* in 1968 where he covers national news. Johnston co-authored *The Working White House* and *Jonestown Massacre*, and is a three-time winner of the White House News Photographers Association Photographer of the Year Award and many other honors. In 1983, he won an Alicia Patterson Fellowship from *Newsday* to cover social and economic change in America.

Boris Kaufman
Soviet/Moscow
Kaufman graduated from the journalism faculty at Moscow State University and joined the staff of the Novosti Press Agency as a correspondent in 1961. Since 1977 he has been a correspondent for *Moskovskiye novosti (Moscow News)*. The awards he has received include a Gold Medal from World Press Photo and a Silver Medal from Interpressphoto.

Yuri Kaver
Soviet/Moscow
A graduate of the Moscow Energy Institute, Kaver began his career as an electrical engineer before turning to photojournalism. A specialist in ecology and ethnography, he has worked for the Novosti Press Agency since 1980, and has won numerous awards, including a special Nature prize and a Gold Medal from World Press Photo and a Silver Medal from Interpressphoto.

233

David Hume Kennerly
American/Los Angeles, California
Winner of the Pulitzer Prize in 1972 for his feature photography in Vietnam, Kennerly was President Ford's official White House photographer from 1974 to 1977. Kennerly was awarded the Overseas Press Club's Olivier Rebbot Award in 1986 and is currently a contract photographer for *Time* magazine. The author of an autobiography, *Shooter,* Kennerly also directed a 30-minute dramatic film, *Bao Chi,* for the American Film Institute.

Los Angeles   1962

Douglas Kirkland
Canadian/Los Angeles, California
Kirkland is one of the world's best known glamor and personality photographers. Twenty-five years in the business have included camera work with Marilyn Monroe, Judy Garland, Barbra Streisand and Christie Brinkley. He was one of the founding members of Contact Press Images and currently works with Sygma Photos. His portfolio will be published by Collins Publishers in 1988.

Vyacheslav Kiselyov
Soviet/Moscow
A member of the Novosti Press Agency since 1987, Kiselyov has worked as a photojournalist for the past 20 years. He is the recipient of awards from Interpressphoto and various national and international exhibits during the past 10 years. He is the author of several books, and once traveled over 60,000 miles around the perimeter of the USSR for a story on Soviet border guards.

Gennadi Koposov
Soviet/Moscow
Koposov is currently head of the photo division of *Ogonyok* magazine. His work as a correspondent has taken him to Finland, Vietnam, Senegal, Sri Lanka, Australia, the Arctic and Antarctica—the last two places featured in his book, *On Two Poles.* Koposov is also the co-author with Lev Sherstennikov of two books on the art of photojournalism. He has shown his work throughout Eastern Europe, in Moscow and Washington, D.C., and has won various awards from World Press Photo, Interpressphoto and other international competitions.

Yuri Korolyov
Soviet/Moscow
Korolyov first took up the camera while stationed at the front during World War II. A graduate of the Institute of Cinematography in Moscow, he has worked for the newspaper *Sovetsky Soyuz (Soviet Union)* since 1959. He spent two months in America in 1967 as a guest of *Life* magazine, and also published in *Sports Illustrated, Time* and *People.* Korolyov has served three times on the jury of the World Press Photo competition.

Pavel Krivtsov
Soviet/Moscow
Krivtsov worked in the city of Belgorod as a special correspondent for the newspaper *Sovetskaya Rossiya (Soviet Russia),* and since 1986 has been on the staff of *Ogonyok* magazine. He is a prize winner in many Soviet and foreign photographic competitions and exhibitions.

Steve Krongard
American/New York, New York
Krongard's work ranges from the real to the fantastic, both on location and in the studio. His advertising and corporate clients include American Express, IBM, Kodak, AT&T, Polaroid and many others. His editorial pictures have appeared in most major American and European magazines.

Bangladesh   1979

Jean-Pierre Laffont
French/New York, New York
Laffont attended the prestigious School of Graphic Arts in Vevey, Switzerland prior to serving in the French army during the Algerian War. He is a founding member of the Gamma USA and Sygma photo agencies, and since 1973, has been a partner at Sygma. He is the recipient of awards from the New York Newspaper Guild and the Overseas Press Club of America, and has received the Madelein Dane Ross Award, the World Press General Picture Award and the Nikon World Understanding Award. His work appears regularly in the world's leading news magazines.

Vladimir Lagranzh
Soviet/Moscow
Vladimir Lagranzh studied at Moscow State University and at the Institute of Journalism. He started his career with the TASS News Agency in 1959, and joined the newspaper *Sovetsky Soyuz* in 1963. A frequent participant in Soviet and international photo exhibits, he has received a variety of medals and diplomas.

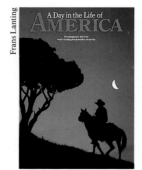
A Day in the Life of America 1986

Frans Lanting
Dutch/Santa Cruz, California
A freelancer who works for *National Geographic, GEO* and other magazines, Lanting also has several books to his name and is the recipient of awards from World Press Photo, Pictures of the Year and the American Society of Magazine Photographers.

Sarah Leen
American/Philadelphia, Pennsylvania
A graduate of the University of Missouri School of Journalism, Leen has been on the staff of the *Philadelphia Inquirer* for five years covering stories in Monaco, Lebanon and South Africa. For the past three years, she has been a member of the faculty of the Missouri Photo Workshop. In 1986, she received an honorable mention in the Robert F. Kennedy awards for her story on Alzheimer's disease.

Andy Levin
American/New York, New York
Andy Levin is a magazine photojournalist living in New York City. His photographs have appeared in magazines including *Life, National Geographic, People* and *Parade.* He has reported on a wide range of subjects from Nebraska farmers to rap musicians. He was awarded top honors in the National Press Photographers Association Pictures of the Year competition in both 1985 and 1986.

Saudi Arabia   1976

Gerd Ludwig *West German/New York, New York*
A founding member of the Visum Photo Agency in Hamburg, Ludwig is a regular contributor to *GEO, Life, Zeit Magazin, Stern, Fortune* and other magazines. He is a member of Deutsche Gesellschaft für Fotografie. On May 4, 1986, just two days after the shooting of *A Day in the Life of America,* he married photographer Dana Fineman. Two hundred of the world's best photojournalists were on hand to cover the wedding.

Aleksandr Makarov
Soviet/Moscow
Aleksandr Makarov has photographed subjects ranging from hospitals to oil pipelines, but his favorite theme has always been ballet, and he has closely followed and recorded the careers of such famous Soviet dancers as Natalya Bessmertnova, Yuri Grigorovich, Maris Liepa, Nadezhda Pavlova and others. A correspondent for the Novosti Press Agency since 1962, his work has been exhibited in both Eastern and Western Europe, and his books on ballet have been published in the USSR, USA, Yugoslavia, Italy, Switzerland, England and Japan. Makarov has received over 50 awards, including the Golden Eye at the World Press Photo competition in 1986.

Oleg Makarov
Soviet/Moscow
Oleg Makarov started his working career as an agricultural mechanic until he joined the newspaper *Leningradskaya pravda* as a professional photographer in 1963. Since 1968 he has been with the Novosti Press Agency. He has won awards throughout Europe and is the recipient of the World Peace Council Prize at the Interpressphoto exhibit in Syria.

A Day in the Life of America   1986

Mary Ellen Mark
American/New York, New York
The winner of numerous awards and grants, Mark has exhibited and published her work throughout the world. In 1985, she won the Robert F. Kennedy Award and in 1986, the Philippe Halsman Award for Photojournalism from the American Society of Magazine Photographers. Her work appears regularly in *Life, The Sunday Times* (London), *Stern, Vanity Fair* and *The New York Times.*

Stephanie Maze
American/Rio de Janeiro
Since 1979, Maze has been a freelance photographer for National Geographic and has worked in the US, Mexico, Spain, Portugal, Costa Rica, Puerto Rico and Brazil. Winner of several California and Washington Press Photographers awards, she has covered three Olympic Games and is currently working in Latin America for several American and foreign publications.

Wally McNamee
American/Washington, D.C.
During his 30-year career as a photographer, Wally McNamee has worked for *Newsweek* and *The Washington Post.* He has photographed more than 100 *Newsweek* covers and is a four-time winner of the Photographer of the Year Award from the White House News Photographers Association in addition to many other honors.

Bhopal   1984

Dilip Mehta
Canadian/Toronto, Ontario
An international photojournalist and member of Contact Press Images, Mehta has covered such diverse subjects as the Bhopal tragedy and political developments in India, Pakistan, the USA and Afghanistan. Mehta's pictorial essays have been published in *Time, Newsweek, GEO, Bunte, The New York Times, Paris-Match, Figaro, The Sunday Times* (London), and other major publications around the world. He has won two World Press Gold Awards and the Overseas Press Club Award.

Claus C. Meyer
West German/Rio de Janeiro
A member of the Black Star photo agency, Meyer was selected in 1985 by Communication World as one of the top ten annual report photographers in the world. His color work has been recognized by Kodak and Nikon, and in 1981 he won a Nikon International Grand Prize. He has published several books on Brazil.

Corneliu Mocanu
Rumanian/Bucharest
Mocanu is one of Rumania's best-known photographers and a member of Agerpress, the Rumanian press agency. He has received many honors and was named International Master of Photography at the Interpressphoto competition in 1983. His work has been published throughout Europe and in the Soviet Union, the United States, Australia, Japan, Iran, Iraq and Kuwait. He participated in *A Day in the Life of the Soviet Union* while preparing his third one-man show.

Aleksandr Mokletsov
Soviet/Moscow
A musician by training, Mokletsov is a graduate of the State Conservatory. He served in the photo reporting division of the Soviet armed forces during World War II, and received four decorations and five medals.

Rogelio Moré
Cuban/Havana
Moré was born in Havana and is a graduate of the San Alejandro school of painting. A photo correspondent for the Cuban news agency AIN, he has participated in various exhibits and competitions and has been honored twice by the Cuban Ministry of Culture for his work.

Jan Morek
Polish/Warsaw
Morek is a reporter for the Polish Press Agency, Interpress. He has participated in international exhibits and in 1987 won an award from World Press Photo. Morek's most important books of photos include, *Poland: The People and Country,* (1978), *Ordinary Poland,* (1980) and *Warsaw* (1985).

Anatoli Morkovkin
Soviet/Moscow
Morkovkin has worked in newspapers, television and radio. He joined the staff of the TASS News Agency in 1979, and has participated in the World Press Photo, Interpressphoto and Bi-photo competitions.

A Day in the Life of America   1986

Matthew Naythons
American/San Francisco, California
A working journalist and physician, Naythons has spent most of his career alternating between photo coverage of world events for *Time* magazine and emergency room duty in San Francisco. In 1979, he founded an emergency medical team to care for Cambodian and Thai refugees. His photographic work appears regularly in major magazines.

Seny Norasingh
American/Raleigh, North Carolina
Norasingh, originally from Laos, now works in Cary, North Carolina. He freelances for *National Geographic* magazine. He previously worked for *The Raleigh News and Observer, The Gastonia Gazette* and *The Daily Advance.* He was twice named North Carolina News Photographer of the Year.

Graeme Outerbridge
Bermudian/Hamilton
Named the 1985 Young Outstanding Person of the Year in Bermuda, Outerbridge has exhibited his work in New York, Washington D.C., London, Boston and Helsinki. His photographs have been published in a variety of magazines including *Vogue* and *The New Yorker.* His first book was *Bermuda Abstracts,* and he is currently working on a new book about bridges.

Vladimir Perventsev
Soviet/Moscow
Perventsev graduated from the philology department of Moscow State University in 1954, and started his career as a print journalist for various Soviet publications before turning to photography. He has worked at the Novosti Press Agency since 1961, and has entered various Soviet and international photo competitions. Perventsev has exhibited his work in the USSR, Hungary, Czechoslovakia, Bulgaria, Angola, Mali, Burkina Faso and Algeria.

Bill Pierce
American/New York, New York
Pierce is a contract photographer for *Time* magazine and is represented by the international photo agency, Sygma. A Princeton graduate, he won the 1983 Overseas Press Club Olivier Rebbot Award for his international photo reporting in Belfast and Beirut. In addition to *Time,* Pierce's work has appeared in *Life, Paris-Match, The New York Times* and *Stern.*

Valeri Plotnikov
Soviet/Leningrad
A graduate of the Institute of Cinematography, Plotnikov is a freelance photographer based in Leningrad. He has shown his work throughout the Soviet Union as well as in Hungary, Czechoslovakia, Bulgaria and the United States, and has received honors from competitions in Bulgaria, Spain, Czechoslovakia and the USSR. Plotnikov is celebrated for his portraits of Soviet actors, directors, artists and musicians.

Sergei Podlesnov
Soviet/Moscow
From 1961 to 1985 Podlesnov worked as head artist at *Semya i shkola (Family and School)* magazine. In 1985 he graduated from the journalism institute affiliated with the Union of Journalists of the USSR and became a correspondent for the magazine *Rabotnitsa, (Woman Worker).* He is currently with the newspaper, *Moskovskiye novosti (Moscow News).*

Aleksandr Polyakov
Soviet/Moscow
Polyakov is a graduate of the journalism faculty at Moscow State University. He has worked in the press since 1976 and joined the Novosti Press Agency in 1983. Polyakov is the recipient of a World Press Photo Gold Medal in 1986.

Larry C. Price
American/Philadelphia, Pennsylvania
Price is currently the director of photography for *The Philadelphia Inquirer's Sunday Magazine.* He previously worked for *The El Paso Times* and *The Fort Worth Star-Telegram.* Since the beginning of his photography career in 1977, Price has won two Pulitzer Prizes: in 1981 for his coverage of the Liberian coup and in 1985 for his photographs of Angola and El Salvador. Price's work has also been honored by the Overseas Press Club, World Press Photo awards and the National Press Photographers Association.

Nikola Radosevic
Yugoslavian/Belgrade
One of the best-known photographers in Yugoslavia, Radosevic is an editor at *Fotografia a Video,* the magazine of the Federation of Professional Photographers of Yugoslavia, of which he is the president. He is also founder and vice president of the Federation of European Photographers. The recipient of over 75 awards, Radosevic was recently honored by the United Nations for his work.

A Day in the Life of Canada   1984

Roger Ressmeyer
American/San Francisco, California
A Yale graduate, Ressmeyer has photographed covers and feature stories for *Smithsonian, People, Time, Newsweek* and *Life.* His work has also appeared on the covers of dozens of books whose authors include Shirley MacLaine, Danielle Steele, Patti Davis and John DeLorean. The founder of Starlight Photo Agency in San Francisco, Ressmeyer has won numerous awards for his portraiture as well as for his coverage of high technology and fashion.

Jim Richardson
American/Denver, Colorado
Currently a special projects photographer for *The Denver Post,* Richardson has published essays on his native state of Kansas in *Life, American Photographer* and *Country Journal.* He was given special recognition in the World Understanding Award in 1975, 1976 and 1977.

Vladimir Rodionov
Soviet/Moscow
Rodionov has worked as a correspondent for Novosti Press Agency since 1972. He has covered Bulgaria, Hungary, Algeria and Afghanistan, and his work has won awards from World Press Photo, *Freie Welt* magazine, Great Wall of China and other international photo competitions.

Galen Rowell
Japan   1985

Galen Rowell
American/Albany, California
Galen Rowell is an environmental photojournalist who has written and photographed seven large-format books as well as doing assignments for *National Geographic* and *Sports Illustrated,* among others. He received the 1984 Ansel Adams Award for landscape photography and has had numerous one-man shows including a 1987 three-month exhibit at the Smithsonian. His most recent book is *Mountain Light: In Search of the Dynamic Landscape.*

Viktor Rudko
Soviet/Tallin, Estonian SSR
Rudko has been on the staff of the TASS News Agency in Tallin since 1971. He is the recipient of a variety of national photo competition prizes and has participated in the World Press Photo, Interpressphoto and other Soviet competitions. He exhibited his work in Finland in 1986.

Sebastiao Salgado
Brazilian/Paris
An international economist by training, Salgado is associated with the Magnum photo agency. His work has appeared in *Time, Paris-Match, Stern, The Sunday Times* (London) and *Fortune.* His ongoing study of the indigenous peoples of Latin America was recognized with the Eugene Smith Award in 1982. He also won a World Press Award in 1984 for his coverage of Ethiopia. His latest book, *The Other America,* was recently published in the United States by Pantheon.

Sergei Samokhin
Soviet/Moscow
Samokhin started working at the Novosti Press Agency in 1979, first in the photo labs and then as a correspondent. He is considered one of the rising talents of Soviet photojournalism.

Bernd-Horst Sefzik
East German/Berlin
A member of the East German Union of Graphic Artists, Sefzik has shown his work in West Germany, Cuba, Hungary, the USSR and in Paris. He is the recipient of the Banner of Labor and other photographic awards.

Aleksandr Sentsov
Soviet/Moscow
Sentsov is a graduate of the Moscow Printing Institute and has worked at the TASS News Agency since 1973. He has received awards for his work from Interpressphoto, Biphoto and *Freie Welt* magazine among others.

Lev Sherstennikov
Soviet/Moscow
Sherstennikov has worked for the newspaper *Literaturnaya gazeta (Literary Gazette)* and, since 1962, at *Ogonyok* magazine. He has also appeared on Soviet television as host of the photography program "Freeze, moment," and he is on the board of editors of the magazine *Sovetskoe foto (Soviet Photo).* Sherstennikov's pictures have been widely published, and he is the co-author with Gennadi Koposov of two books on photojournalism. He has participated in Soviet and international photo competitions, and shown his work in Poland and Laos.

Neal Slavin
American/New York, New York
The recipient of numerous awards, Slavin is published regularly in *The Sunday Times* (London), *Stern, GEO, Town & Country, Newsweek* and *Connoisseur.* His work has appeared in one-man and group shows and his latest book is *Britons.*

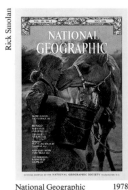
Rick Smolan
National Geographic   1978

Rick Smolan
American/New York, New York
Project co-director of *A Day in the Life of the Soviet Union,* Smolan also created with David Cohen *A Day in the Life of Australia* (1981), *A Day in the Life of Hawaii* (1983), *A Day in the Life of Canada* (1984), *A Day in the Life of Japan* (1985) and *A Day in the Life of America* (1986). Prior to these extravaganzas, Smolan was a full-time photojournalist whose work appeared in major publications including *Time* and *National Geographic.*

Feliks Solovyov
Soviet/Moscow
Solovyov has taken photographs since childhood, professionally since 1959. A freelancer who works in all genres, he has published his photos in many Soviet publications as well as with AP and such western magazines as *Stern, Der Spiegel* and *Quick.*

Yuri Somov
Soviet/Moscow
Somov is a graduate of the Higher Institute of Photography who has worked as a correspondent for the Novosti Press Agency since 1958. He has covered over 60 countries, photographing heads of state, astronauts, Olympic games and sports championships. Somov is the recipient of various awards, including five Gold Medals, in competitions in Switzerland, Czechoslovakia, Bulgaria, Mexico, Hungary and other countries.

Andrew Stawicki
Canadian/Toronto, Ontario
After working as a staff photographer in Frankfurt for *Bild Zeitung* and in Warsaw for *Swiatowid,* Stawicki joined *The Toronto Star* in 1983. He has won several prizes in Poland and Holland and has exhibited his work in Poland and Canada.

George Steinmetz
American/San Francisco, California
A graduate of Stanford University in geophysics, Steinmetz dropped out to spend two and one-half years hitchhiking through more than 20 African countries. His work appears regularly in *Fortune, Forbes, GEO, Mother Jones* and *The New York Times Magazine.* He is currently working on an assignment for *National Geographic* magazine on oil exploration.

Vladimir Syomin
Soviet/Moscow
Syomin has been interested in photography for "as long as I can remember," but spent many years of travel and work in other fields before achieving his professional dream. After seven years at the Novosti Press Agency, he quit publishing to become a freelance photographer, often working with the Moscow youth weekly *Sobesednik (Companion).* He is a regular participant in the World Press Photo and other competitions.

Patrick Tehan
American/Santa Ana, California
A photo published in *A Day in the Life of America* earned Tehan top honors in the magazine division of the National Press Photographers Association Pictures of the Year competition. In 1981 Tehan was named as a regional Photographer of the Year by the N.P.P.A. He is currently on the staff of the *Orange County Register* in Santa Ana, California.

Jan Tikhonov
Soviet/Riga, Latvian SSR
Tikhonov works for the Novosti Press Agency in Riga, Latvia and was named Honored Worker of the Latvian SSR. He has received over 100 citations from international competitions including the Grand Prix in the Man and the Sea competition in Poland. In 1987 he was awarded the Gold Medal in a major exhibition in Moscow for his color photo, "Latvian Folk Dancer."

Tomasz Tomaszewski
Polish/Warsaw
Tomasz Tomaszewski is vice president of the Union of Polish Art Photographers. His work appears in many international publications such as *National Geographic, Paris-Match, Stern, Domenica Christiana* and *La Vie.* His book, *Remnants—The Last Jews of Poland,* was published in the United States in 1986 and in Switzerland in 1981. His photographs have been exhibited in Poland, France, Sweden, Canada and the USA. He has won several prizes in Poland and France.

Magsarym Tserenzhamts
Mongolian/Ulan Bator
Tserenzhamts has been a professional photographer, specializing in photojournalism, for 20 years. He is the recipient of the Grand Prix Award from Interpressphoto and various medals from competitions in Moscow, Ulan Bator, Prague, Tokyo, Berlin and Havana. A Laureate of the Union of Mongolian Journalists, he works for the newspaper *Unen* in Ulan Bator.

David C. Turnley
American/Detroit, Michican
Turnley has been a *Detroit Free Press* staff photographer since 1980. He is currently working on a project for *National Geographic* and *The Detroit Free Press* on Afrikaners. His work from South Africa won a citation in 1986 from the Overseas Press Club for best newspaper reporting from abroad. For each of the past four years, Turnley's coverage has won or been cited for best photo reporting by the Overseas Press Club. In 1986 he won three World Press Photo awards including the Oscar Barnack Award, and the Canon Essayist Award.

Peter Turnley
American/Paris
Turnley studied at the University of Michigan, the Sorbonne and the Institut d'Etudes Politiques in Paris before becoming a photographer. He is now a contract photographer in Paris for *Newsweek,* covering Europe, the USSR, North Africa and the Middle East. Turnley, who published a book, *A Food Lover's Guide to Paris,* has had exhibits in the United States and France and has been the recipient of several French photography awards. In 1986 he was cited by the Overseas Press Club for his international coverage.

Jerry Valente
American/New York, New York
Valente specializes in hotel advertising, but his work includes editorial and corporate assignments and industrial annual reports. His photos have appeared in *A Day in the Life of America ,* and he hopes awards await him in the future.

Viktor Velikzhanin
Soviet/Moscow
Velikzhanin's grandfather and father were both photographers, and he started his own career as a photojournalist with the TASS News Agency in 1968. In recent years he has extensively covered the Soviet art world, and has given a series of lectures on photography at Moscow State University. Velikzhanin received a Gold Medal from Interpressphoto, a Bronze Sport Ambassador of Peace Award, and was a participant in World Press Photo.

Yuri Vendelin
Soviet/Tallin, Estonian SSR
Vendelin began his professional career in photography in 1973 and has worked as a correspondent for the TASS News Agency in Tallin since 1974. He has been a participant and award winner in Soviet and international exhibitions including World Press Photo and Interpressphoto, and has had a show of his work in Finland.

John Vink
Belgian/Brussels
A member of VU in Paris, Vink has been a freelance photographer since 1971. His work appears in *Time, Le Monde* and *Liberation,* and he is currently involved with personal projects on Italy and the African Sahel. His photographs have appeared in 30 group and solo shows in Europe. In 1986, he was the recipient of the Eugene Smith Award.

Afghanistan 1985

Vladimir Vyatkin

Vladimir Vyatkin
Soviet/Moscow
Vyatkin has worked at the Novosti Press Agency, first as a designer and then as a correspondent, since 1968. In 1985 he was named an International Master of Press Photography by the International Organization of Journalists, and was winner of the USSR Union of Journalists Prize for the same year. His numerous awards include both the Golden Eye and the Gold Medal from World Press Photo in 1986, as well as top honors from the Interpressphoto and Great Wall of China competitions. Vyatkin is also an instructor at the journalism faculty of his alma mater, Moscow State University.

Grace Kennan Warnecke
American/New York, New York
Warnecke is a freelancer who photographs primarily for film and television production. Fluent in Russian, she has worked extensively in the Soviet Union, with Senator Edward M. Kennedy, Joan Baez, ABC and Metromedia, and she has also covered the Moscow Olympics for *Newsweek.* Warnecke has had three one-woman shows in San Francisco and took first prize in a photo competition on the performing arts.

Lajos Weber
Hungarian/Budapest
Weber began his photographic career in 1967. Since 1979 he has worked as a reporter at MTI, the Hungarian Press Service. Weber specializes in sport and political reporting and has successfully participated in many international photo competitions, receiving awards from World Press Photo and Interpressphoto. In 1986, he was awarded first prize at the Goodwill Games for his photo, "Sports—the Bridge of Peace."

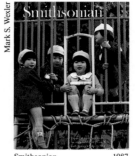
Mark S. Wexler
Smithsonian 1987

Mark S. Wexler
American/New York, New York
Mark Wexler travels the world as a photographer for a variety of editorial and corporate clients including *Time, Life, Smithsonian* and *GEO.* He won three World Press Photo awards for his work on *A Day in the Life of Japan.*

Marina Yurchenko
Soviet/Moscow
After two years of work in the geography faculty of Moscow State University, Yurchenko decided to pursue a career in photojournalism. She has worked for *Sputnik* and the weekly *Moskovskiye novosti (Moscow News),* and has been a correspondent for the Novosti Press Agency since 1981. Yurchenko counts among her photographic specialties art, theater, religion and daily life.

Contributing Photographers

Viktor Akhlomov *(Izvestiya)*
Soviet/Moscow

Michael Benson *(freelancer)*
American/New York

Gary Eisenberg *(freelancer)*
American/Miami, Florida

Pat Field (*National Geographic***)**
American/Washington, D.C.

Aleksandr Gushchin
(Sovetsky Soyuz)
Soviet/Moscow

Nikolai Ignatiev *(freelancer)*
Soviet/Moscow

Viktor Kornyushin
(Moscow Patriarchate)
Soviet/Moscow

Vladimir Pcholkin *(freelancer)*
Soviet/Moscow

Roman Poderni *(TASS)*
Soviet/Moscow

Ivan Sirota
(Moscow Patriarchate)
Soviet/Moscow

Mikhail Romanov
(Moscow Patriarchate)
Soviet/Moscow

Aleksandr & Grigori Tombulidis
(freelancers)
Soviet/Tbilisi, Georgian SSR

Aleksandr Zemlyanichenko
(Sovetsky Soyuz)
Soviet/Moscow

Ira Shapiro
Associate Publisher
Shapiro is the founder and president of American Showcase, Inc., which publishes an extensive collection of photography, illustration, and graphic design books, magazines and one of the world's top-selling graphics annuals. Formerly a curator of the Nikon Gallery in New York, and a co-founder of *Photograph* magazine, it was Shapiro's concern with his daughter Josslyn's recurring nightmares of nuclear war that prompted his significant role in the negotiations that led to cooperation between Collins Publishers and Novosti Press Agency.

Staff Members

Produced and Directed by:
David Cohen and Rick Smolan

Associate Publisher
Ira Shapiro

General Manager
Cathy Quealy

Associate Director
Patti Richards

Art Director
Thomas K. Walker
GRAF/x

Sales Director
Carole Bidnick

Collins Publishers, Moscow

Assignment Editors
D. Gorton
Bill McCabe
Mark Rykoff
Grace Warnecke

Editorial Coordinator
Torin Boyd

Chief Writer
Jean-Christophe Castelli

Logistics & Text Coordinator
Lew Stowbunenko

Debriefing Coordinator
Devyani Kamdar

Collins Publishers, Madrid

Travel Coordinator
Karen Bakke

Film Traffic Coordinator
Jennifer Erwitt

Data Coordinator
Amy Janello

Editor
Brennon Jones

Support Staff
Laura Lowenthal
Marie-Claire Rodriguez Dulin
Juan Galiano Casas
Rusty Conway
Fernando de Miguel
Miriam Hernández
Milagros Bello

Collins Publishers, New York

Director of Finance and Administration
Stanford Hays

Sales Manager
Debbie Donnelly

Finance Manager
Melanie Miller

Administrative Assistant
Clio McNichol

Bookkeeper
Marian Yates

Research

Research Coordinator
Mark Rykoff

Research Assistant
Marie Stock

Writer
J. Curtis Sanburn

Research Consultants
Professor Donna Bahry
New York University
Dr. Jack Kollmann
University of California, Berkeley
Professor Nancy S. Kollmann
Stanford University
Tamalyn Miller
Harriman Institute, Columbia University

Copy Editor
Grace Deutsch

Design and Production

Assistant Art Director
Beth A. Crowell

Production Manager
Stephanie Sherman

Design Assistance
Alan Baseden

Production Assistance
Fiona L'Estrange
Carole Sessler

Map Design
Brian Sisco

Picture Editing

Director of Photography
Arnold Drapkin
Time Magazine

Picture Editors
Don Abood
The Picture Group
Anatoli Bogomolov
Novosti Press Agency
Mark Grosset
Rapho Agency
Kent Kobersteen
National Geographic Magazine
Eliane Laffont
Sygma Photos
Aleksei Pushkov
Novosti Press Agency
Dieter Steiner
Stern Magazine
Yuri Zodiev
Novosti Press Agency

Associate Picture Editors
Ruth Eichhorn
Burda Magazine
Alfonso Gutiérrez
A.G.E. Fotostock
Stephanie Maze
Woodfin Camp & Associates

Advisors

Publishing
Oscar Dystel

Legal
E. Gabriel Perle
Proskauer, Rose, Goetz & Mendelsohn
F. Richard Pappas
Paul, Weiss, Rifkind, Wharton & Garrison

Business
Phillip Moffitt

Advisors, Moscow
Felix Rosenthal
Time Magazine
Viktor Khrolenko
Nicholas Louis

Novosti Press Agency
Valentin Falin
Chairman
Sergei Ivanko
First Deputy Chairman
Georgi Fedyashin
Deputy Chairman
Vladimir Milyutenko
Deputy Chairman
Anatoli Bogomolov
Director, Photography Department
Yuri Zodiev
Director, Public Relations Department
Konstantin Vertiporog
Deputy Director, Public Relations Department
Yuri Karpukhin
Deputy Director, Public Relations Department
Vladimir Verbenko
Deputy Director, Photography Department
Boris Vlasov
Senior Editor, Photography Department
Boris Polkhovski
Director, Western Section, Public Relations Department
Valeri Golubtsov
Editor, Western Section, Public Relations Department
Anelya Yanovich
Editor, Photography Department

Novosti Publishing House
Aleksei Pushkov
Director
Vyacheslav Kiktev
Deputy Director
Sergei Nikitenko
Director, Public Relations Department
Yuri Arsenev
Deputy Head, Foreign Manuscript Department
Eugene Zykov
Senior Editor

Dai Nippon Printing Co., Ltd.
Takeshi Fukunaga
Vice President, New York
Kimio Honda
Project Manager, New York
Ryo Chigira
Project General Manager, Tokyo
Fumiya Chiba
Project Manager, Tokyo
Kosuke Tago
Project Assistant Manager, Tokyo
Kikuo Mori
Separation Dept.
General Manager, Tokyo
Yuichiro Sato
Separation Dept.
Associate Manager, Tokyo

William Collins Sons & Co., Ltd. (London)
Ian Chapman
Chairman
George Craig
Vice Chairman
Sonia Land
Group Finance Director

Collins' Sales Representatives

Mid-Atlantic
Robert Eickermeyer
John Liebfriend, Jr.
Bert Lippincott, Jr.

Midwest
Charles Boswell
Wes Caliger
Ted Heinecken
Louis Livengood
Mary Rowles
Gordon Slabaugh

Mountain States
Gordon Saull

New England
Joan Emery
Marc Seager

Southeast
Edward Springer
Edward Wood, Jr.

Southwest
Theron Palmer
Brian Sumrall
Chuck Weeth

West Coast
Jonathan Hager
Ted Lucia
William Maher
Robert Ditter

Agents

Canada
Steve Pigeon
Chris Moseley
Mike Fisher
Masterfile, Stock Photo Agency
415 Young St., Ste. 200
Toronto, M5B 2E7
Phone (416) 977-7267
In Vancouver (604) 734-2723
In Montreal (514) 935-7901

France
Annie Boulat
Cosmos
56 Boulevard de la Tour Maubourg
75007 Paris
Phone (1) 4705 4429
Telex 203085

Hong Kong
Stock House
310 Yue Yuet Lai Bldg.
43-55 Wyndham Street
Hong Kong
Phone (5) 220486 or 224073
Telex 78018

Italy
Grazia Neri
Via Parini, 9
20121 Milano
Phone (2) 650832 or 650381
Telex 312575

Japan
Bob Kirschenbaum
Pacific Press Service
CPO 2051, Tokyo
Phone (3) 264-3821
Telex 26206

Spain
Alfonso Gutiérrez Escera
A.G.E. FotoStock
Buenaventura Muñoz, 16, entlo.
08018 Barcelona
Phone (93) 300-2552
Telex 51743

West Germany
Marita Kankowski
Focus
Moorweidenstr. 34
2000 Hamburg 13
Phone (40) 446-3769
Fax (40) 45 6804

United Kingdom
Terry Le Goubin
Colorific!
Gilray House, Gloucester Terrace
W2 London
Phone (01) 723-5031 or 402-9595
Telex 943763

Sponsors and Contributors

Sponsors
Eastman Kodak Company
Pan American World Airways
Nikon, Inc.
Sony Corporation of America
Intourist

Contributors
Academy of Sciences of the
    USSR
Aeroflot
Apollo Stationery Co., Inc.
Apple Computer Inc.
Bolshoi Theater
Casa Carril, S.A.
Concorde International Travel
Contact Press Images
Carnase, Inc.
Dynamac Computer
    Products, Inc.
Exhibition of Economic
    Achievements of the USSR
    (VDNKh)
Fisher Pen Company
Gamma Press Images, Tokyo
Gosagroprom (State Committee
    for Agricultural Production
    and Industries)
Gosteleradio (USSR Television
    and Radio Committee)
Horizon Type
Iberia Airlines
Image Photographic Laboratory
Intercongress
Izvestiya
Ken Lieberman Laboratories
Komsomolskaya pravda
Life Magazine
Lightspeed
Clyde McWilliams Studio, Inc.
Mezhdunarodnaya Hotel,
    Moscow
MicroStore
Mirror Technologies
Modern Age Photography
Moscow Central Pioneer Palace
Moscow City Council of Trade
    Unions
Moscow News
Moscow Patriarchate of the
    Russian Orthodox Church
Moskovskaya pravda
Mossoviet (Moscow City
    Council)
Nakhimov Naval Academy,
    Leningrad

National Geographic Magazine
Newsweek Magazine
N.Y. Film Works
Ogonyok Magazine
Professional Business
    Resources, Inc.
Qantas Airways Limited
Schneider/Erdman Laboratory
Sobesednik Magazine
Sovetskaya kultura
State Cinematography
    Committee of the USSR
Sun Microsystems
SuperMac Technology
Suvorov Military Academy,
    Moscow
Sygma Photos
TASS
The Chase Manhattan Bank
    N.A.
The Supreme Court of the
    Soviet Union
The Tomanskaya Infantry
    Division, Moscow
Time Magazine
US-USSR Trade and Economic
    Council
USSR Bank for Foreign
    Trade
USSR Ministry of Atomic
    Energy
USSR Ministry of Automobile
    Production
USSR Ministry of Civil Aviation
USSR Ministry of Culture
USSR Ministry of Health
USSR Ministry of Railroads
USSR State Traffic Inspection
    (GAI)
Vladimir Prison
Warp Nine Engineering
Woodfin Camp & Associates
Yuri Gagarin Cosmonaut
    Training Center

Friends, Advisors and Consultants

Irakly Abashidze
Chingiz Aitmatov
Viktor Akhlomov
Marina Albee
Anatoli Alekseyev
Feliks Alekseyev
Vladimir Alekseyev
Gennadi Alferenko
Tony Allison
Juan Angel Alonso Alonso
Wyatt Andrews
Dmitri Ardamatsky
Sen Arevshetyan
Peter Arnett
Herbert & Dorothy Ascherman
Tamara Ashikhmina
Edvard Aslanyan
Donna Bahry
Andrei Baidak
Mikhail Bakhmetyev
Elena Baranova
Joyce Barnathan
Agustín Barrenechea-Arando
Aleksei Batashev
John & Anne Bedford-Lloyd
Kallibek Bekzhanov
Aleksei Belekov
David Bell
Vladimir Belyaev
Vladimir Belyakov
Alla Belyakova
Raymond & Shirley Benson
Oleg Benyukh
Amin Berdyev
Gussie Bergerman
Georgi Bezhanidze
Andrei Bezruchenko
Britt Blaser
Gene Blumberg
Abe Blumenfeld
Zoya Boguslavskaya
Celestine Bohlen
Mikhail Bolysov
Liz Marie Bond
Irina Borovko
Aleksei Borzenko
Erik Boyd
Candes Bregman
Bruce Brizzolara
James Brown
David Brown
Humphrey Bruno
Axel Buchhold
Andrei Budakov
Alexei Budyonny
Yevgeni Bugaenko
Sergei Bykovsky
Dan Campi
Antonio Cañete López
Ken Carbone
David Carriere
Martha Casanave
Juan Castro
Andrei Chernoshchyok
Judy Ann Christensen
Albert Chu
P.N. Chuprynov
Jesse & Rhoda Claman
Jim Clancy
Daniel Cohen
Gail Cohen
Norman & Hannah Cohen
Sandy Colton
Vicki Comiskey
Mike Contard
Jack Corn
Robert Cromer
Harriet Crosby
Emilio de la Cruz
Maxine Curry

ose Maria Cuspinera
obyn Davidson
rancisco Delgado Francisco
Natalya Derevyanko
Mikhail Derevyanko
David Dickes
Carmela "Chicky" Dioguardi
Vladimir Dobkin
Anatoli Dobrynin
Sheila & Brennon Donnelly
Mary Donovan
Natasha Driskell
Gene & Gayle Driskell
Yuri Dubinin
Dick Duncan
Vladimir Dzhanibekov
Mark & Lois Eagleton
Dr. Richard & Mina Eisenberg
Jeff & Susan Epstein
Elliott Erwitt
Gladys Esparza
Barbara Essick
Luis Expósito Poyato
José Luis Fabá Soldevila
Jason Farrow
Svyatoslav Fedorov
Gerry Feil
Harlan Felt
Terry Ferrante
Adam Frank
Wilbur E. Garret
Bill Giordano
Russell Glick
Dr. Raymond & Bette Goldblum
Joseph Goldin
Tankred Golenpolsky
Valentin Golovko
Andrei Goncharov
Ma. Victoria Gorbeña
Mark Gorelik
Bill & Mary Agnes Grant
Vladimir Grigoryev
A. Grinevich
ken Gukaszyan
Aleksandr Gurevich
Volodin Guseinov
Pyotr Gustyr
Inge Hacker
Lee Harris
Nick Harris
Robert & Ginny Heinlein
Mariano S. Hernández González
Jim Hickman
Will Hooper
Will Hopkins
Richard Horowitz
Stephen Hull
Pashazada Allahshukur
   Hummatoglu
Frederique Ibon
Isabella Ibragimov
Varvara Igushenya
Georgi Ilyichev
Anatoli Ilyukhov
David Imedashvili
Vern Iuppa
Viktor Ivanov
Daniil Iyeromonakh
James Jackson
Rick Jacobs
Carmen Jaime
Juan Jiménez
Steve Jobs
Sandra Johnson
Nancy Jones
Nicolas Jones
Janie Joseland
Bill Joy
Lorraine Kacaba
Dmitri Kalinin
Prabhakar P. Kamdar
Galina Karagodina
Nijazi Karakashly
Yelena Kashirina
Viktoriya Kasparova
Vazgent Katolikos

Diane Kay
Valeri Kazyulin
Jay Kennedy
Batyr Khalliev
Gai Khanov
Sergei Kharchenko
Aleksandr Khatkin
Mikhail Khazanov
Yevgeni Khazanov
N. E. Khoroshilov
Yorie Kiriyama
Lyubov Kizilova
James Klein
Glenn & Nancy Knowlton
Tanya & Natasha Kolodzei
Anatoli Komrakov
Yelena Konovalova
Anatoli Korchevsky
Viktor Koretsky
Boris Korolev
Vitali Korotich
Vladimir Kostygin
Igor Kovalets
Natalya Kovtoun
Sergei Kozlov
Enn Kreem
Andrew Kruger
Anya Kucharev
Rudolf Kucherov
Arkadi Kudrya
Yuri Kuidin
Oleg Kulesh
Yuri Kupin
Vladimir, Tanya & Yelena
   Kurbakov
Col. Anatoli Kurchin
Kaku & Sumiko Kurita
Vera Ladonnikova
Valentin Lazutkin
Johannes Mikhkel Leas
Martin Levin
James & Lynn Levinson
Tanya Levitskaya
Olivia Lichtenstein
Ken Lieberman
Lightspeed
Aleksei Lipovetsky
Aleksandr Lisyansky
Linda Little
Esteban Llagostera
Edward & Anne Lloyd
Tom & Susan Lloyd
John Loengard
José Luis López
Richard LoPinto
Ed Lowe
Viktoriya Lyudvikovskaya
Spuds Mackenzie
Timothy Madden
Abdulla Magomedov
Anatoli Makarov
Evelyn Malave
Pyotr Malinovsky
Dmitri Mamatov
Ambassador & Mrs. Jack
   Matlock
Richard & Lucienne Matthews
Holloway McCandless
Jason McManus
Jack McTaggart
Michael Mears
Elmar Medler
Sergei Merkulov
Evelyn Messinger
Archbishop Methodius
Vitautas Mikulicius
Ida Mintz

Pam Miracle
Valeri Miroshnichenko
David Mishur
Vladimir Molchanov
Igor Monichev
Art Mont
Juan Morales
Dayse Biscaro Moreira
Akio Morita
Valeri Morozov
Sergei Morozov
Ann Moscicki
Bruce Mowery
Rinat Mukhamadiev
Karen Mullarkey
Dulce Murphy
Lon Murphy
Tom Nagorski
Mikhail Nakoryakov
Carmela Naval
Leonid Nedopekin
Igor Nemira
Valeri Niyazmatov
Obeidullah Noorata
Askar Numanov
Aurora Nuñez
Tim O'Meara
Dan O'Shea
Ulumgi Ochirov
Jacqueline Ochs
Karlen & Tamara Oganesyan
Gevorg Oganesyan
Susan Oglesby
Kadyrkul Omurkulov
Oleg Orlov
Jim Osborne
Nikolai Osipov
Yevgeni Osipov
Sergei Ostroumov
Bill Pakela
Elizabeth Palladino
Guy Palmer
Eduardo Paramio Roca
Enrique Paredes
Jack & Gertie Parker
Ann Pasque
Igor Pavlov
Yelena Pavlova
Vladislav Pavlunin
Valeri Pechennikov
Viktor Pereiko
Aleksei Perevoshchikov
Elizabeth Perle
Edward Perper
Mario Perrone
Vladimir Pervukhin
Nancy Pfister
Iosif Pikarevich
Patriarch Pimen
Boleslav Pinchuk
Carl Pite
Metropolitan Piterim
Aleksandr Plekhanov
Sergei Polyakov
Elizabeth Pope
Boris Popov
Nikolai Popov
Germán Porras
Joan Powell
Viktor Prusakov
Cherie Quaintance
Kisana Raiganad
Suzanne Rees
Ed Reingold
Spencer Reiss
Igor Reutenko
Aleksandr Revin
Stephen Richards
Maksim Rilsky
Rodney Robson
Angel Rodríguez
Nikolai Romanov
Jim Rosemary
Terry Rosen
Cynthia Rosenberger
Mikhail Roshchin
David Rudman
Pedro Ruiz

Anatoli Rybakov
Vladimir Rychalin
Mikhkel Saare
Boris Sadekhov
Nola Safro
Oleg Sakharov
Marianne Samenko
Kai Sanburn
Fernando Sánchez
Jonathan Sanders
Dugar Sanzhyev
Valeri Sapegin
Gennadi Savkin
Murray Sayle
Kenny Schaeffer
Steve Scheier
Fred Scherrer
Dr. Leonard & Millie Schwartz
Leonard Sclafani
John Scully
Miguel Segovia
Eve Sehested
Vladimir Sergeyev
Kay Sexton
Vladimir Shatalov
Vyacheslav Shcherbakov
Kristin Sherlaw
Aleksandr Shevelyov
Rimi Shiraishi
Leonid Shkolnik
Aleksandr Shlyakov
Rasim Shukyurov
Valeri Shumakov
Mikhail Sigov
Aleksandr Simchenko
Bob Siroka
Mariya Sitkina
Richard E. Smith
Rick Smith
Temple Smith
Leslie Smolan
Marvin & Gloria Smolan
Sandy Smolan
Aleksei Smolentsev
Aleksandr Sokolov
Veniamin Soleyev
Tatyana Solomatina
Joy Solomon
Sergei Solovyov
Mark Johan Soosaar
Irina Sotnikova
Kim Spencer
Helen Sprowls
Vasili Starovoitov
Jim Stockton
Georgi Stoilik
Jocelyn Stoller
John Stossel
Admiral Lev Stolyarov
Viráj & Daniel Stowbunenko
Joe Strear
Anatoli Stuk
Ralph Subbiondo
Nadezhda Sukhanova
Konstantin Sukharev
Yuri Surkhaikhanov
Lidiya Svobodina
Asit Talukder
Mark Taplin
Vladimir Tarabashchuk
Sovet Tatambayev
Levan Tedyashvili
Tamara Tereshchenko
Leonard Terlitsky
Vadim Tetevin
Irina Timokhina
Valeri Timonin

Antonio de Toro
Andrei Trofimuk
Gennadi Tsarkov
Sergei Tselovalnikov
Yuri Tserenkov
Dmitri Tulchinsky
William Turnley
Stepan Tyuntenev
Yuri Tyurin
Vladimir Ulyanov
Oleg Uralov
Nabikhan Utarbekov
Mikhail Vaik
Ulugbek Vakhabov
Inessa Valk
Della Van Heyst
Neil Vanderdussen
Carlos Vaquero
Viktor Varlen
Ignacio Vasallo
Marina Vasilyeva
Konstantin Vavilov
Félix Vázquez
Jaroslav & Lois Verner
Aleksandras Vielavicius
Natalya Villa-Landa
Aleksandr Vinogradov
Nikolai Vishnevsky
Marina Vivier
Vladimir Vlasov
Aleksandr Vorobyev
Vitali Voronov
Igor Voznesensky
Av Westin
Eric & Lael Weyenberg
Carole Williams
Dave Winer
Matthew Winokur
Peter Workman
Robin Wu
Larry Wyner
Linda Wyner
Yegor Yakovlev
Yuri Yefremov
Aleksandr Yemelyanov
Viktor Yerin
Aleksandr Yevreinov
Jennifer Young
Viktor Yukechev
Valeri Zaitsev
Olga Zameskina
Vladimir Zaretsky
Yuri Zemmel
Yuri Zenyuk
Captain Sergei Zhambochyan
Viktor Zhuravlyov
Veniamin Zinovyev
Pyotr Zubkov
Natasha & Anastasia Zykova
Dmitri Zyubanov

and very special thanks
to: Raymond H.
DeMoulin of Kodak,
Dwayne O. Andreas &
James Giffen of the
US-USSR Trade &
Economic Council and
Ed Acker & Jeff
Kriendler of Pan Am
without whom this
book would not have
been possible.

Lev Sherstennikov

Thank you to all the homes and schools, factories and collective farms, cities and villages of the Soviet Union that opened their doors to our photographers.